P9-CSV-095

ALL ABOUT The Ice Age

ALL
ABOUT

The
Ice Age

by **Patricia Lauber**

foreword by **William L. Donn**

with maps and drawings by
John C. Wonsetler and
12 pages of photographs

RANDOM
HOUSE
NEW YORK

allabout
books

SECOND PRINTING

© COPYRIGHT, 1959, BY PATRICIA LAUBER

All rights reserved under International and Pan-American Copyright Conventions.
Published in New York by Random House, Inc., and simultaneously in Toronto,
Canada, by Random House of Canada, Limited.

LIBRARY OF CONGRESS CATALOG CARD NUMBER: 59-6461

MANUFACTURED IN THE UNITED STATES OF AMERICA

Contents

The photograph section begins on page 53.

Foreword

Our earth is several billion years old. During most of this time, the climate over the world as a whole was warmer than now. But several times during these billions of years climates became cold and ice spread over much of the world.

As you will find from this book, the last great Ice Age, which occurred during the past million years, actually consisted of four separate glacial stages. During the tens of thousands of years between the glacial stages, the climate was quite warm; and it was during these interglacial periods that early man developed.

Did the end of the fourth glacial stage about 11,000 years ago mark the end of the great Ice Age? Or is a fifth glacial stage still to come? Will a thick layer of ice again cover much of our world?

There is still very much that we must learn in order to answer these questions, as well as another one: Why did the Ice Age begin in the first place?

Miss Lauber tells much that scientists have learned already. She includes the fascinating story of how Louis Agassiz proved to the world that there really was an Ice Age during which ice covered so much of the world. This is one of the great discoveries of modern times. Perhaps another such discovery will settle the problem of the ice ages of the future.

WILLIAM L. DONN

Lamont Geological Observatory
Columbia University

1
The Mystery

Slowly—inch by inch, foot by foot—the ice crept southward. From the far north, great sheets of ice spread out, swallowing the land. From the high mountains, rivers of ice reached down with frigid touch.

All things gave way before the ice.

Ice carved its way through rock. It scoured the sides of mountains. It gouged the earth. It snatched up dirt, gravel, stones, and boulders. Whole forests fell, trees snapping like toothpicks before the advancing ice.

There was snow, falling in howling blizzards. There was rain that fell and froze. The mass of ice grew several thousand feet thick. And, growing, it pushed farther south. Year after year it flowed forward. Forests, meadows, lakes, and hills vanished beneath the ice.

Its presence was felt far away. For frigid winds swept off the ice, bringing winter to the lands ahead. Before the cold, all living things fled or perished.

And this went on for thousands of years.

Sometimes the ice would melt at the edges and draw back. Then the advance would start again. Creeping, grinding, scouring, gouging, the ice of ever-winter would swallow the land.

Finally the great tongues of ice, the great sheets of ice, retreated for good, leaving behind gigantic floods of melt-water.

In time, life came back to the land. For the ice was gone. It had drawn back to the far north, back to the mountain heights.

The land, of course, was changed. There were new lakes and rivers, born of melting ice. Ice had sculptured hills and valleys. There was land scoured bare. There was land made rich by soil the ice had dropped.

On this ice-free land, plants grew and spread. Animals came to live on it. And men followed the animals.

Thousands of years went by. Men made the land theirs. They grazed herds, planted crops, and built cities where once sheets of barren ice had glittered in the sun. And no one guessed the wintry secret of the past.

The reason is not hard to understand.

Glaciers, those huge masses of ice, lay only in far places. What reason was there to think that ice a thousand or more feet deep had once covered a fourth of the world's land? So, for thousands of years, the earth held its secret.

At last, the mystery began to unfold. First, scientists learned to read the clues. They learned that in another age ice had ruled the land. Like detectives, they pieced together evidence to draw a frightening picture of a different world.

But each new discovery seemed to open up other mysteries. How had the ice grown? How had it moved? And, most puzzling, *why* had glaciers grown and spread?

For years scientists have sought the answers to those questions. Seeking, they have climbed the highest mountains. They have camped on lonely fields of ice. They have drilled and probed and had themselves lowered into ice. They have lived on ice islands in the Arctic Ocean. They have braved the coldest places on earth.

The more they learn, the more they need to know. For there are signs that we are now moving toward another ice age.

Will great sheets of ice again swallow North America and Europe? We cannot know for sure until we have solved the mystery of the Ice Age. Somewhere, still hidden in it, is the key to the future.

Much work lies ahead. The Ice Age is a very old mystery. And man's efforts to solve it began only 150 years ago, when scientists first learned the meaning of some curious rocks.

2
Glaciers Move!

Long before men knew anything about glaciers, they had noticed certain curious rocks, which were strewn over northern Europe, the British Isles, Switzerland, and other nearby areas. The rocks themselves were perfectly ordinary stone. The strange thing about them was that they didn't belong in the places where they were found.

A big boulder might be the only rock of its kind in the whole region. Some boulders made of one kind of rock were embedded in a completely different kind of rock. Some were perched in strange positions, as if a careless giant had laid them down and forgotten them. Because the boulders didn't belong, they were named *erratics*, meaning "wanderers."

Then there were vast blankets of sand and gravel, called *drift*. The drift didn't belong where it was found either.

Clearly, erratics and drift had been brought into the regions where they were found. But how?

For hundreds of years, men puzzled over this question. The most widely believed theory was that a flood had brought them in. Men thought a giant and sudden flood had swept across the land, carrying erratics and drift. When the flood ended, the rocks were left behind.

In the early 1800's, a new idea was put forward. Suppose, some men said, the rocks were carried by ice. Suppose glaciers once reached down from the mountains, then melted and dropped the rocks.

The idea seemed ridiculous to most people. But two men took it seriously. They were a pair of Swiss scientists named J. Venetz and Jean de Charpentier. Studying glaciers high in the Swiss Alps, they came to believe that this was indeed what had happened.

A glacier dropped this great rock on a mountainside.

Swiss glaciers, they said, had once grown tremendously. The ice moved down into valleys and onto plains. It carried along boulders, sand, and gravel. Later the ice melted, dropped its rocks, and retreated to the mountains.

Most people simply scoffed at the idea. Growing, moving glaciers? Never! Everyone knew that these great rivers of ice existed only in the mountain heights. They didn't move and they didn't change. They stayed the same year after year after year.

7

Among the doubters was a young Swiss scientist named Louis Agassiz. Agassiz was not a geologist, a scientist who studies the earth. His science was zoology, the animal kingdom. His special field was fishes, both living and fossil, and he was famous for his brilliant studies of the fossil remains of ancient Brazilian fishes. By the age of 29, he had set about the enormous job of studying and classifying all fossil fishes.

Just at this time, though, his interest was caught by the theory of his two friends, Venetz and Charpentier. Their idea didn't sound likely to Agassiz. But, like all scientists, Agassiz had a great deal of curiosity. He was also an athletic young man who enjoyed climbing mountains. He decided to spend his summer vacation exploring glaciers. Perhaps he could show his friends where their theory went wrong.

In the summer of 1836, Agassiz went up the valley of the River Rhône. His way led him far up the Alps to the mighty glacier that, by its melting, fed the Rhône. With the skill of a mountaineer, he began to climb up, over, and around the huge, glittering mass of ice.

What he saw convinced him that *he* had been wrong. Glaciers did move. Venetz and Charpentier were right, except that they hadn't gone far enough. Studying clues,

Agassiz came to believe that a great ice age had once occurred. Glaciers in the Alps and elsewhere had grown tremendously. As a result, the Alps, northern Europe, and the British Isles had been overrun by a sea of ice.

These ideas plunged Agassiz into a whole new field of science. He became the world's first Ice Age detective— and possibly the greatest one the world has ever known.

In the winter of 1837 he went back to the Alps. Before he could prove the Ice Age, he had to prove that glaciers did move—and had moved.

Everywhere he looked, he saw signs of moving glaciers. He saw rocks polished and grooved by existing glaciers; where there were no glaciers, he saw rocks with exactly the same marks. (See illustration on page 55.) Surely they must have been polished and grooved by glaciers of the past! At the ends and sides of glaciers, he found tumbled piles of rock, called *moraines;* where there were no glaciers, he found similar piles.

The marks and moraines could mean only one thing. Glaciers moved, growing and shrinking. The same marks and moraines could be found far from Alpine peaks. So at one time the glaciers must have spread out from the Alps.

But this was still theory, not proof. Agassiz's mind

Agassiz set up his headquarters by a Swiss glacier.

was filled with questions that had to be answered. What had caused these great masses of ice? What changes had taken place in them? Where had they gone? How had they affected the places around them? How did they move? How fast did they move? Had the glaciers changed in size? How thick had they been? How thick were they now?

The main problem was where to start. Agassiz decided to find out how thick a glacier was. He and some friends strapped lengths of iron rod to their backs. Then they climbed the glacier of Aar to make a boring and measure its thickness. They hadn't brought enough rod. They went back for more, but it still wasn't enough. So they went back again. This time Agassiz managed to satisfy himself that the glacier was about 1,000 feet thick.

He tackled another question: Did glaciers move? A few people thought so. Most people said no, for glaciers seemed the same from year to year.

Agassiz felt sure that glaciers moved. How else would rocks and valley walls become grooved and polished? How else would moraines be built up? But he needed proof.

He decided to sink a row of stakes across a glacier. If they moved, this would prove the glacier moved. If they stayed where he had put them, the glacier would not have moved.

The test was an excellent one. (It is still used today.) But the first experiment failed. Agassiz had driven the stakes five or six feet into the ice. And five feet of surface ice melted during the summer. The stakes lost their support and fell flat on the ice. Agassiz had not learned anything about glacier movement. But he had learned something about melting.

By this time, Agassiz had made public his theory. It was based partly on his own studies, which convinced him that glaciers had once reached far down from the mountains and the Arctic. In part, he drew on the findings of scientists in another field. These men had been digging up fossil remains of ancient animals and plants. The fossils showed that Europe had once been much warmer.

Agassiz put all this information together. Then he announced that the world, long ago, had gone through a great ice age. In it, massive glaciers had reached down from the Alps to the plains. And a vast sheet of ice had reached from the Arctic to central Europe and Asia.

He described the Ice Age as a time when "Siberian winter established itself" over lands that had been green with plants and alive with animals. "Death," he said, "enveloped all nature in a shroud" of rock-hard ice. The erratics and drift, so long a puzzle, had been carried along by the ice, then left behind.

It was a bold theory—and a staggering one. Who could believe that glaciers had once grown so? That these green lands had once been sheathed in ice? That whole species of plants and animals had vanished, never to be seen again? The mind could not take in this strange picture of an icy world.

The leading geologists were outraged. For one thing, if Agassiz was right, then *their* theories were wrong. For another, Agassiz wasn't even a geologist. He was a zoologist. What could he know about glaciers? They advised him to stick to his fossil fishes.

Agassiz was doing just that. He was hard at work on his big project. But he could not keep away from glaciers. He *had* to know more about them.

The summer of 1839 again found him scaling the Alps. On the glacier of the Rhône, he came upon a cabin built by a scientist-priest in 1827. The cabin was known, but Agassiz was startled to find it where he did. Somehow, in twelve years, the cabin had moved 4,000 feet down the glacier from the place where the priest had built it. Had the cabin moved by itself? Or had the glacier moved 4,000 feet and carried the cabin with it?

The next summer Agassiz went after the answer. He again tried the experiment of driving stakes into the Aar glacier. This time he hammered them in to a depth of 18 feet. They formed a straight line across the ice. Agassiz checked their position against certain rocky points on the valley wall.

When he returned in the summer of 1841, Agassiz at last had the answer. Glaciers did move! The stakes had moved down the valley. What was more, they had moved at different rates. The straight line had taken the shape of a broad U. This showed that the center of the glacier moved faster than the sides. Later experiments gave the same results. Glaciers moved. And the rate at which they moved could be measured.

The same experiment told Agassiz a good deal about the giant splits that appear in glacial ice. These splits are called *crevasses*, and they are huge. They may be hundreds of feet wide and perhaps a mile long. Often snow bridges a crevasse, hiding the great split. (See photograph on page 58.) Many a man has plunged to his death through a thin snow bridge.

In Agassiz's time, everyone knew about crevasses. But no one knew what caused them. Agassiz saw they were produced by glacial movement. The huge mass of flowing ice sometimes met a big obstacle, like a hill. It had to flow over or around the obstacle. And this tore the ice open. (See photograph on page 56.)

Agassiz piled up more and more information. Spurred on by the need to know, he scaled mountains that had defeated many climbers. Laden with equipment, roped to the rest of his party, he floundered through snow. With footholds cut by guides, he climbed sheer faces of ice. He leaped small crevasses. He edged his way over big ones on bridges of ice. For there is only one way to study a glacier—get out on it.

The information Agassiz brought back was causing a great stir in scientific circles. There were those who still scoffed at him. But some geologists were beginning to listen—and believe.

Agassiz went to Britain for a scientific meeting. As soon as possible, he went off to explore the countryside. He felt sure there must be signs of long-vanished glaciers. And there were. Pleased, but not surprised, he wrote a detailed account of his findings. A number of famous British scientists were won over.

Back Agassiz went to the Alps, the only place he could study living glaciers. This time he wanted to find out whether water flowed from glaciers in winter.

Certain geologists now agreed that glaciers moved. But they explained it this way. The earth's central heat, they said, melts the bottom of the glacier. Melting causes the glacier to slide.

Agassiz didn't believe that. But there was only one way to find out—go and see. If these geologists were right, the glacier would melt in winter as well as summer. And if it melted in winter, water would flow from it.

Agassiz climbed to the Aar glacier in the cold of March. In summer, water poured over its surface. Now the surface lay white and still. More important, no water was flowing into river beds from the bottom of the glacier. Search as he might, Agassiz could find no sign that the bottom of the glacier was being melted.

Then what did cause glaciers to move? Agassiz didn't know. But perhaps he could learn something from the inside of a glacier. Summer found him back on the ice, drilling deep holes in it.

Agassiz decided he was not learning enough this way. He would go down into the glacier himself.

It was an adventure that almost killed him.

In the ice were several deep holes, made by streams that poured into them. Agassiz diverted a stream so that it no longer ran into its hole. Then, seated on a kind of swing, he had himself lowered into the hole. Down, down the icy tube he went. At 80 or 100 feet down, light still came through the ice. Agassiz was fascinated by the blue bands that ran through the ice. What could they be?

He was so absorbed that he didn't notice what was happening. Suddenly his feet plunged into icy water. He shouted in alarm. But he was 125 feet down, and his

Agassiz found himself dropping into icy water.

cry was muffled. The men on top thought he wanted to be lowered. They payed out more line. Agassiz was dropped into the freezing water. This time no one could mistake his cries. The men hastily hauled him up from the water that would have frozen him.

At the end of that summer, Agassiz climbed to the top of the Jungfrau—almost 14,000 feet high. It was a tremendous and dangerous climb. But Agassiz wanted to study weather conditions. They produced the snows that made glaciers. The study could be made only at a great height. So Agassiz made the climb.

A few years later, Agassiz summed up his studies in two books. He said he had lived with glaciers, striving "to draw from them the secret of their formation and advance." And so he had. His books gave the world its first understanding of ice as a major force on the earth.

Meanwhile, he had finished his book classifying fossil fishes. And his fame as a zoologist brought him an invitation to lecture in Boston.

Agassiz accepted with enthusiasm. He sailed for the New World in the fall of 1846, landing at Halifax, Nova Scotia. "Eager to set foot on the new continent so full of promise for me," he later wrote, "I sprang on shore and started at a brisk pace for the heights above the land." Almost the first things he saw were grooved and polished rocks—the marks of glaciers. Ice had also invaded North America. Agassiz had been sure this must be so. Now he had proof.

Though he had come to lecture, Agassiz stayed in America. He became one of the leading zoologists in the United States. But he could not get glaciers out of his mind. Wherever he traveled, he looked for their marks, looked for clues to the Ice Age that had swallowed parts of North America, Europe, and Asia.

In North America, he found, an enormous ice sheet had overrun mountains, hills, valleys, and plains. He said, "The polished surfaces stretch continuously over hundreds and hundreds of miles. . . . Scratches, grooves, and furrows are unbroken for vast distances."

One journey took Agassiz to Brazil. There, in the valley of the Amazon, he found thick green tropical growth. And under this—the marks of glaciers (from an even earlier ice age).

His imagination leaped back to a time when, in a cold world, huge masses of snow had piled up around the poles. As it grew 12,000 to 15,000 feet deep, he said, pressure changed the snow to ice. And then the ice began to reach out toward parts of the world where animals roamed green lands.

That strange time of ever-winter has fascinated men since Agassiz first described it. And many scientists have taken up the trail of glaciers in the Ice Age. They have added to Agassiz's findings; they have corrected some. But Agassiz remains a towering figure in the field. He was the first man to prove that glaciers move, the first to read the clues that led straight to the Ice Age.

3

When the Ice Reached Down

The Ice Age began perhaps a million years ago, perhaps less. It did not strike the world like a giant blizzard, but came on slowly, over a long period of time.

It was born in the cold places of the earth—near the poles and among the heights of lofty mountains. Here snow fell and did not melt. That is, some melted. But the rate of snowfall was greater than the rate of melting. So the snow piled up, year after year.

New snow falls as fluffy crystals. But as more snow falls on top of it, that weight packs the crystals together. In time, they become ice. You have probably seen much the same thing happen on a stretch of busy sidewalk after a snowfall. The parade of feet packs the snow down into a hard, ice-like substance. This is what happens when a glacier builds, except that the snow eventually becomes rock-hard ice. In fact, ice is a kind of rock.

So, where snow fell and did not melt, great masses of ice built up. After a time, by their own weight, the masses of ice began to flow.

Probably ice first grew on the cold, high lands of Antarctica. Here it took the form of an icecap. As the center weight built up, the ice flowed outward in all directions. It became a vast, moving sheet of ice, which is called a *continental glacier*.

But the Antarctic ice sheet had little effect on the world. Antarctica is surrounded by sea, and glaciers do not form over the sea. So this ice did not spread out over neighboring lands. Instead, as giant tongues of ice reached the sea, their ends broke off. These floated away as icebergs. (See photograph on page 64.)

In the north, ice seems to have grown first on the high plateau of Greenland. (It could not have started at the North Pole because the Pole is surrounded by water.) From the highlands, glaciers in the form of a huge ice sheet spread into North America.

At the same time, ice was forming in the Alps and in the mountains of Scandinavia. A mountain glacier took the form of a glittering white, broad river of ice. It covered the valley floor and reached hundreds of feet up the valley walls. (See photograph on page 53.)

Mountain glaciers flowed down through the valleys. Beyond the valleys was land. The ice crept out upon it.

MONTREAL

MINNEAPOLIS

MILWAUKEE

DETROIT

BOSTON

DES MOINES

CHICAGO

CLEVELAND

PHILADELPHIA

NEW YORK

CINCINNATI

ST. LOUIS

Where the ice reached
in North America
during the Ice Age

Another ice sheet formed in western Siberia. Spreading westward it crossed the Urals and flowed into the mass of ice in Scandinavia.

At the height of the Ice Age, a massive icecap covered Greenland. Northern Europe was locked in the grip of a huge ice sheet that flowed south from Scandinavia. Ice covered parts of Russia, Siberia, and Asia.

In North America the ice stretched far south. Its traces have been found in New Jersey, Missouri, and Nebraska. Our western mountains lay under small icecaps and mountain glaciers.

In North America alone, ice covered nearly six million square miles of land. All told, ice lay heavy upon 27 per cent of the world's land—more than 15 million square miles. In places the ice was several thousand feet thick.

And most geologists believe that this enormous growth of ice took place not once but four times during the Ice Age. Four times the ice advanced. Four times it melted and retreated, the fourth time for the last time.

Where had all this ice come from? It came, in a sense, from the oceans.

All ice begins as water, and the oceans are vast reservoirs of water. The heat of the sun draws water into the air. Winds blow it landward. The warm, moisture-laden air meets colder air over the land. The cold causes the moisture to condense and fall as rain or snow.

Normally, rain (or snow) in time flows back into the oceans. But when the glaciers were building, this did not happen. The snow and rain became ice—and stayed ice. This meant that an enormous amount of the world's water was locked up in ice. Ocean levels dropped as much as 300 feet.

As a result, new land appeared. There were new coastal areas, new islands, and land bridges. Britain was probably joined by land to the continent of Europe. A land bridge linked Siberia and Alaska.

Far to the south of the icy wilderness, a great change also took place. In some way, the Ice Age seems to have forced rain-bearing winds south. And these made deserts bloom with life.

During the Ice Age, the southwestern United States was wetter and cooler. The brown-gray deserts of today were green. And in Africa, the Sahara, tamed by rain, was a green and fertile land where men and animals could live.

Then, when the Ice Age ended, so did the rains. The

green vanished, to be replaced by desert brown.

To the north, there were floods. For when the ice melted an immense amount of water was freed. Some flowed immediately back into the oceans. Some collected on land areas in the form of inland seas and lakes.

The biggest of these lakes covered parts of Minnesota, North Dakota, Manitoba, Ontario, and Saskatchewan. It was bigger than all our Great Lakes together. But this giant lake vanished, draining away through the Minnesota River to the Mississippi. We know of it only because we can trace its shore line and bottom.

Other lakes changed their shapes and sizes. Some drained away, only to form new lakes. The Great Lakes are descended from a whole series of lakes that formed when the last ice sheet melted.

In some places, glacial lakes remained and can still be seen today.

Ice and floods left behind a much changed land. Ice had carved mountains and valleys, made or destroyed hills. Ice and floods had shifted the beds of rivers, in some cases even reversing the course of rivers. Old lakes had vanished and new ones appeared. The boundaries of land and sea had changed. Some land had been made richer, some poorer.

The earth was changed—and so was life. Ice and climate had wiped out whole species of plants and animals. They had forced others to migrate or adapt. For before the ice all living things had to flee or perish.

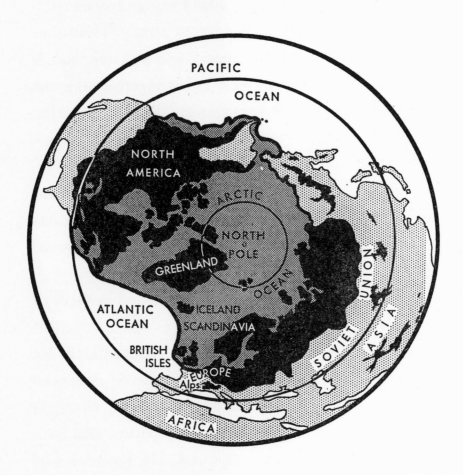

The ice sheets covered much of Europe, Asia, and North America.

4

Life in
the Ice Age

A million years ago elephants crashed through the forests of North America. Herds of camels, bison, deer, and antelope roamed the plains. Saber-toothed tigers lurked in ambush, crouching to spring at a passing horse or deer. Giant, shaggy-coated ground sloths uprooted trees and ate their leaves. The land was alive with wolves, lions, wild pigs, bears, and dozens of other animals.

Then the Ice Age came upon the world. By its end,

three-fourths of all these animals had vanished from North America. Some are still found in other lands, but many are long vanished from the face of the earth.

The Ice Age began in places far removed from trumpeting elephants and snarling tigers. But its effects on life were drastic.

To begin with, there was the ice itself, creeping relentlessly forward, building up hundreds or even thousands of feet deep. Forests fell like grass before the advancing wall of ice. Meadows, plains, hills, and all that grew on them disappeared beneath the ice. Wherever ice lay for thousands of years, life ceased to exist.

Then there was the cold that moved before the ice, carried ahead by winds that swept the glaciers. Over hundreds, then thousands, of years, this advancing cold forced whole zones of plant life south. The northern edge of a zone would die; the southern edge lived—and spread south.

The land nearest the ice was much like the tundra of northern Canada today. Just below the surface lay frozen earth that never thawed. In winter, the top layer was also frozen and dead. But in summer, melt-water from the ice turned the top layer into a bog. Here only mosses, scraggly bushes, and dwarf willows could live.

South of the tundra was a plain of fine, wind-blown soil. It bore a rich crop of grass each year.

South of the plain were the forests. First a northern forest, like the woods that grow today in Maine and Minnesota. Then a more tropical forest.

These were the zones that shifted south. As the ice advanced, plains became tundra. Northern forest became plains. Tropical forest was invaded by trees of the northern forest. And the tropical forest, in turn, spread southward.

When ice released the land, zones of plant life moved north—only to shift south again with the next advance of ice.

Plants are the basic form of food on earth. Many animals eat plants. Other animals eat the animals that eat plants. And men eat both plants and animals.

So, when zones of plant life shifted, animal life shifted also. In the last part of the Ice Age whole groups of people shifted, too. These people were herders and hunters. Where their animals went, they followed. And the animals followed the plants that were their food.

The ice advanced slowly and retreated slowly. But the changing climate, the cold, the floods affected every form of life. Some animals survived by migrating. Some

33

managed to adapt themselves to the cold. Many could not survive the changes. They became extinct, disappearing from the earth.

We know only part of this story. We know that certain mammoths adapted to the cold. Over hundreds of years, their coats thickened until the great beasts were protected by long, shaggy fur. The same thing happened with certain rhinoceroses, which also grew woolly coats. These animals became cold-loving. They hugged the northern boundaries of land, along with reindeer and arctic foxes.

The woolly rhinoceros adapted to the Ice Age.

We know, too, that at some point, certain animals simply died out and are no longer found anywhere. The saber-toothed tiger was one of these. A big, lithe, vicious killer, the saber-tooth ruled wherever he lived. No animal could challenge him. Yet the ice wiped him out.

The giant ground sloth also became extinct. These sloths were cousins of the small sloths that live today in South America. Clumsy and slow-moving, they were bigger than grizzly bears. Their skin was armored with little pieces of bone and covered with thick, long hair. It protected them from many animals, like wolves and

The saber-toothed tiger preyed on other animals.

lions. There is evidence that early men tamed the sloths, which were harmless plant-eaters. The men survived, but the sloths did not.

Yet other animals disappeared from one part of the world but survived in others. Camels vanished from North America. So did horses.

And so, mixed in with what we know, are mysteries that no one has yet solved.

Why did the saber-toothed tiger become extinct?

What happened to the mammoths? We know there were mammoths before the Ice Age. We know woolly mammoths adapted themselves to the cold, to the changes of climate. Why, then, did they die out?

Perhaps the greatest mystery of all has to do with horses.

During the Ice Age, great herds of horses grazed on the grassy plains of North America, Europe, and Asia. In Europe and Asia horses survived both the Ice Age and its end. In America horses vanished completely. Why did this happen?

Many answers have been suggested. Some people have said disease must have wiped out American horses. Others have imagined herds of horses wiped out by flesh-eating enemies. But no reason seems to hold up, for

Ice Age horses of America vanished completely.

where there were horses there were bison. Diseases or enemies that attacked horses would have attacked bison. Yet the bison survived. Whatever the reason, American horses became extinct. And there were no more horses in the Americas until European explorers and colonists brought them here.

There are also great gaps in our knowledge of the people who lived during the Ice Age. We do know that 20,000 years ago, toward the end of the Ice Age, primitive people lived in Europe. They were cave dwellers, and they were skilled hunters and herders. They could not write. But they drew pictures on the walls of their caves, and they made carvings. Their paintings, like their carvings, tell a story of animals. For to these people, animals were both food and clothing.

On the walls of these caves, long-dead animals parade. There are woolly rhinoceroses. There are mammoths and bison and horses. There are lions, bears, hyenas, saber-toothed tigers—animals that wanted the same caves the people lived in.

A whole Ice Age village has been uncovered in Czechoslovakia. Here Ice Age hunters camped. They pitched shelters and warmed themselves with fires. Piles of bones show that they hunted mammoths, rhinoceroses, lions, horses, arctic foxes, and reindeer.

These ancient hunters killed small animals with spears. But they trapped the big ones by digging deep pits and covering them over. When a mammoth or rhinoceros fell into the pit, they killed it with huge stones.

Most of these Ice Age people lived well south of the glaciers. We don't know for sure, but perhaps some

Some Ice Age people used skins for clothing and shelter.

learned to live near the edge of the ice sheets. Certainly, they *could* have. They had the knowledge and skills required to live in a cold land.

They had fire, which they would have needed for warmth. On or near the tundra, they would have found animals—food. From the same animals they could have got warm furs for robes and clothing. With their tools of flint and bone, the people could have made clothing like that worn today by Eskimos.

Fire, food, clothing. The people would have needed one more thing: shelter. There were some caves, but not enough. Still, the people had the skills and tools to make tents. They could have felled and trimmed poles, peeled birchbark. They could have skinned animals, dressed the skins, and laced the skins around tent poles. Would the tents have been warm enough? Quite probably. Similar ones are used by tribesmen today in the icy winter of eastern Siberia.

Did these people live near the edge of the glaciers? Did they see the ice advance or retreat? We don't know, and we may never know. But perhaps the surprising thing is that we know so much. For this is not a story told by boulders and moraines. It is a story that has been dug out of the earth by scientists who study the past.

5
Detectives of Time

Several kinds of scientists study life in bygone ages.

One group is the archaeologists, who dig for ancient cities and towns. They carefully uncovered the Ice Age village in Czechoslovakia. They have explored ancient caves and studied the paintings. They can tell the skills of a primitive people by studying remains of their tools and weapons.

Then there are the fossil hunters, the paleontologists. They are the ones who have told us most about the animals and plants of the Ice Age.

A fossil is the remains of an animal or plant that lived in an ancient era. Fossils can be bones. They can also be impressions in rock of plants, animals, or insects. They can be shells. They can even be footprints.

The world's first great fossil hunter was a Frenchman named Georges Cuvier. In the beginning, Cuvier was particularly interested in the study of living animals. Then, in 1795, he discovered some ancient bones under the soil of Paris. Study of them brought him to an astounding conclusion. They were elephant bones! But they were not like the bones of modern elephants. These bones had belonged to a somewhat different creature— an ancestor of the modern elephant.

You can imagine the surprise that swept Paris. Elephants were animals from faraway lands like Africa and India. Yet here was Cuvier saying that elephants had once roamed northern France. It seemed unbelievable.

Still, Cuvier was a brilliant and famous scientist. His findings could not be ignored. And, in any case, elephant bones were just the beginning.

Fascinated by what he had found, Cuvier went on digging. He dug in Paris. He dug elsewhere in France. Soon he was turning up fossilized remains of fantastic creatures. He found lizards the size of whales. He found

Cuvier discovered bones of prehistoric animals.

lizards that had been able to fly. He found that France had once been home to long-haired elephants (mammoths), hippopotamuses, rhinoceroses, bears, and other huge, odd creatures.

In his study of living animals, Cuvier had learned an

43

enormous amount about their bone structure. He knew how the bones were put together. Now he drew on this knowledge to help him with his fossils. Given as a clue just a few bones, he could figure out what animal this had been, how big it had been, and what it had looked like. He could take a collection of ancient bones and put them together in the shape of the animal's skeleton.

As the strange animals took shape, Cuvier's mind leaped to questions. Why had certain kinds of animals vanished from France? Why had others vanished from the world? How had they been entombed in the earth? When had this happened?

There was only one way to find out—go on digging. And Cuvier did. He also studied mines and quarries, where men had cut deep into the earth.

He began to find a pattern. The fossils were laid down in layers. He found a layer of sea creatures, a layer of fresh-water creatures, a layer of land creatures. The fossils of each group were mixed in with a particular kind of earth. The earth was divided into layers of chalk, soft limestones, clay, sand and limestone, and so on.

The meaning was clear. At various times the Paris region had been invaded by the sea. Between these invasions, it had been dry land dotted with fresh-water lakes and streams. When that was so, the region supported certain kinds of animal and plant life. Their remains formed one layer in the earth. This layer ended when the sea took over the land. Then a layer of the remains of sea creatures and plants was laid down.

Why had the sea advanced and retreated over the Paris region? Because, Cuvier said, "life had often been disturbed by great and terrible events which are everywhere recorded." He believed that the world had been swept by a series of catastrophes—floods, upheavals, and ice. That, he said, was why layers of fossils ended and changed.

Today we know that these great and terrible events did not come suddenly upon the world. Most were slow, creeping changes. But this does not really matter. The important thing was Cuvier's discovery of fossils and their meaning. In his skilled hands, fossils revealed strange beasts of the past. He discovered that fossils occurred in layers. And the layers showed the order of events—first this happened, then that, then something else.

Many fossil hunters have followed Cuvier. They have dug all over the world. Much of what we know about life in the Ice Age comes from their findings. These same findings also tell us about climates and lands of the past.

If an area is rich in fossils of grazing animals, we know that area was a plain. The fossil bones of a hippopotamus mean a forest—and a tropical one. If fossilized wood is spruce, we know the climate in which it grew was cold or temperate. If fossilized wood is palm, the climate here was warm or tropical.

Fossils, then, tell us about ancient life. They tell us about the land and climate. They tell us in what order events occurred. But there is one very important question they do not answer: When? They do not tell us how long ago an animal or plant lived.

Over the years, scientists had to do a lot of guessing. For example, they would study many layers of fossils. They would check with scientists in other fields. When might the mammoth hunters have lived? When did geologists think a certain volcano had erupted? Then they would put all the answers together. From the summing up, they worked out a timetable of events.

According to the timetable, the Ice Age ended 25,000 years ago. Nobody was sure of this date. But nobody could prove it wrong either—until quite recently. Then a new method of investigating the past was developed. Scientists found a way of dating things that happened thousands of years ago.

The new method was used on an Ice Age fossil. And it showed that the last great advance of ice occurred only 11,000 years ago. The Ice Age was much closer to modern times than anyone had even dreamed.

The new means of dating grew out of atomic work. Working with the atom, scientists discovered that certain materials have a kind of built-in clock or calendar. It is possible to use this clock to date events of the far past.

The first such clock was based on a discovery made in the early 1900's. Then scientists found that certain kinds of uranium atoms decay into certain kinds of lead atoms.

That happens because the uranium atoms are radioactive—that is, they give off part of themselves in the form of rays or particles. As they give off rays, they change to lead. And they change at a fixed rate.

The change takes a very, very long time. In fact, it takes 4½ billion years for half of certain atoms in a sample of uranium to change to lead. That is why we say uranium has a half-life of 4½ billion years. At the end of that time, half these atoms will have decayed into lead.

Scientists know how to measure the rate of decay. They can tell exactly how many particles are given off in any period of time.

This, in turn, tells them how long the uranium atoms have been decaying—or how old they are.

Scientists can make similar measurements with other elements that have radioactive atoms.

Using this method, they have been able to say, "This piece of pitchblende is 700 million years old." They have been able to say when a mountain rose and when a sea bottom was formed.

Now, uranium dating is fine for certain kinds of rocks. But it doesn't work with fossils. Another way was needed to date the remains of once-living plants and animals.

In the late 1940's, the way was found by Dr. Willard F. Libby of the University of Chicago. He, too, used a built-in atomic clock. But the key to this clock was radioactive carbon, called carbon-14.

Carbon-14 is formed about five miles out in Earth's atmosphere. Air movement mixes the carbon-14 with ordinary carbon dioxide. In our air there is only a tiny amount of carbon-14—one part of carbon-14 to a trillion parts of ordinary carbon dioxide. But the tiny amount is enough, for carbon-14 can be detected in any sample of carbon dioxide.

All plants breathe in carbon dioxide. So, Dr. Libby reasoned, they must also take in carbon-14. This meant that all plants are slightly radioactive.

Animals eat plants. People eat animals and plants. So, said Dr. Libby, all living things must be radioactive. For all living things must take in carbon-14.

Like the uranium atoms, carbon-14 decays at a fixed rate. But it decays much faster than uranium. Its half-life is a little less than 6,000 years. This means that half its radioactivity is gone after 6,000 years. Half *of the remainder* is gone after another 6,000 years. Half of that is gone after another 6,000 years. Almost all the radio activity is gone after 50,000 years.

How does this help date a fossil?

Well, the amount of carbon-14 in a living tree always stays the same. (The amount that decays is balanced by the amount the tree keeps taking in for as long as it lives.)

When a tree dies, it stops taking in carbon-14. From

then on, the carbon-14 in the tree decays and is not replaced. And it decays at a fixed rate.

Suppose, Dr. Libby thought, we measure the amount of carbon-14 remaining in a dead tree. We can do that with a Geiger counter. This should tell us how long the tree has been dead. For example, suppose it has half as much carbon-14 as a living tree. This should show it has been dead 6,000 years.

Dr. Libby began testing his ideas. He started by working with things whose ages were known. That way he could see how the finding from the Geiger counter compared with the known age.

He used a piece of a dead giant redwood tree; its age had been worked out from the rings in the tree's trunk. A museum director gave him a small piece of wood from the death ship of an Egyptian pharaoh; its age was known from Egyptian history.

In each case, Dr. Libby carefully prepared his material, reducing it to carbon. Then he tested for carbon-14. Finally, he worked out the age. The carbon-14 test worked!

Scientists began to send Dr. Libby material from all parts of the world. Given a piece of charcoal from an ancient fire, Dr. Libby could date the man who had built the fire. Given a bit of linen, he could date the man who had worn the cloth. A whole new timetable began to emerge.

Then, in 1950, someone sent Dr. Libby a piece of fossilized wood from Wisconsin. The wood had once been part of a spruce tree. The tree had grown in a forest near the region now known as Two Creeks. When the last great sheet of ice pushed down from the north, it snapped off the trees in this forest and buried them.

How long had this tree been dead? Most scientists would have said about 25,000 years. But when Dr. Libby used his carbon-14 test, the answer turned out to be 11,000 years.

From Germany, England, and Ireland came other samples of fossilized wood. All had been part of forests snapped and buried by the ice. Dr. Libby ran his carbon-14 test. It seemed to show that the Ice Age ended in Europe about the same time it ended in North America.

Bit by bit, scientists are discovering *what* happened in the Ice Age. Geologists track the path of glaciers. Fossil hunters tell what the ice did to life. Other scientists date events during the last part of the Ice Age.

Meanwhile, a different group of scientists has been hard at work on the question of *how* the Ice Age happened. They are trying to find out more about how glaciers move, a search that has taken them out onto vast and silent fields of ice.

Bradford Washburn (Fairchild Aerial Survey)

Two great rivers of ice, Muldrow Glacier (right) and Traleika Glacier (left), meet on the slopes of Mt. McKinley, Alaska.

Agassiz studied the flow of this glacier in the Swiss Alps. The drawing is from one of his books.

American Museum of Natural History

American Museum of Natural History

Agassiz discovered that these rocks had been polished by a glacier during the Ice Age.

Bettmann Archive

Louis Agassiz (1807-1873) proved that glaciers once covered much of Europe, Asia, and North America.

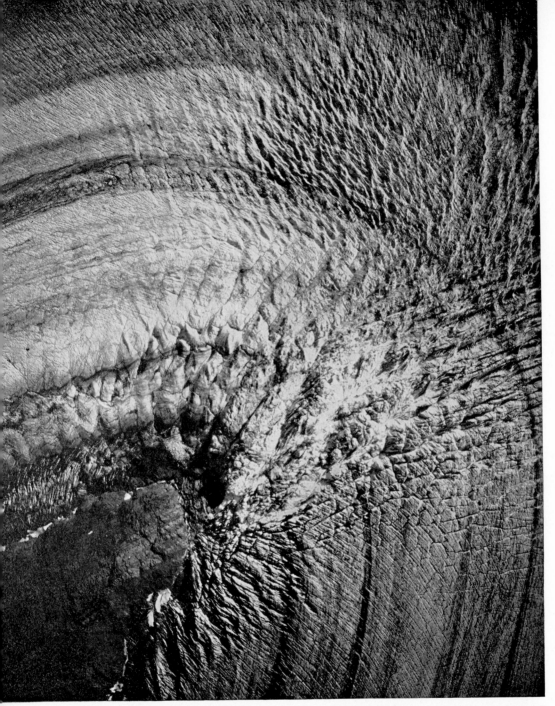

Bradford Washburn (Fairchild Aerial Survey)

When a glacier flows around an obstacle, the ice develops cracks, called crevasses. Shoup Glacier, Alaska, photographed from a mile above.

Geologists survey Lewis Glacier (Kenya) in preparation for an
I.G.Y. expedition. At the right, snow has fallen into a crevasse.

Wide World

U.S. Forest Service

At the melt line, the ice of a glacier turns to water. Crillon Glacier, Alaska.

Through a hole in the snow bridge, scientists in Antarctica have lowered a rope ladder to the bottom of this crevasse.

National Academy of Sciences—I.G.Y.

A glaciologist descends into a crevasse to study its walls more closely. McCall Glacier, Alaska.

National Academy of Sciences—I.G.Y.

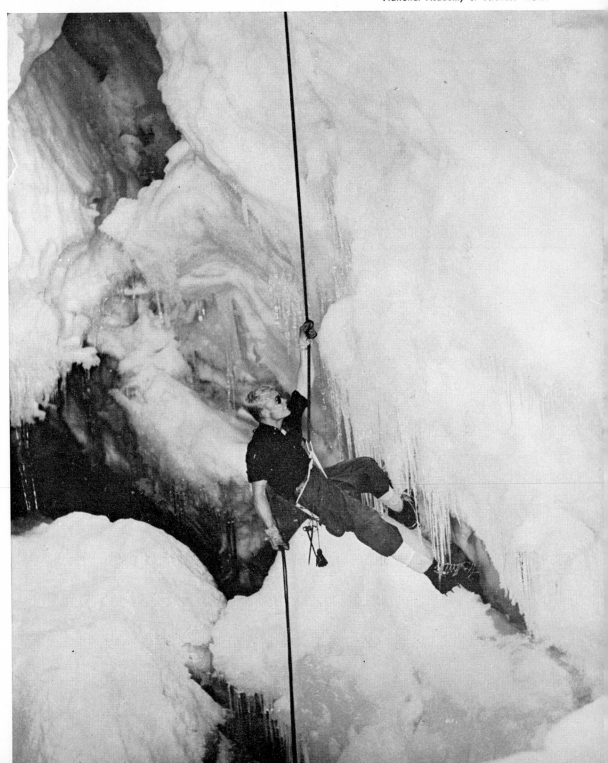

A glaciologist takes an ice core from Blue Glacier at the I.G.Y.
Glaciological Research Station, Olympic Mountains, Washington.

National Academy of Sciences—I.G.Y.

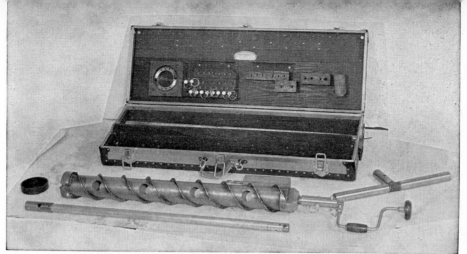

National Academy of Sciences—I.G.Y.

Glaciologists use these instruments to obtain cores from ice and snow.

At the South Pole, a glaciologist uses a carpenter's saw to cut a thick ice core.

Wide World

A scientist at Little America, Antarctica, takes an ice core.

Underwood & Underwood

In Antarctica, two scientists study ice and snow in a shallow pit. On the snow platform are tools used in the study.

National Academy of Sciences—I.G.Y.

U.S. Weather Bureau

This floating I.G.Y. laboratory in the Arctic Ocean, Drift Station A, had to be abandoned when it split apart.

U.S. Coast Guard

This iceberg broke away from a glacier in Greenland. A Coast Guard vessel, on International Ice Patrol. sends warnings for North Atlantic shipping.

6

Exploring Glaciers

The engines of the plane grew fainter and fainter. Within minutes the sound faded away entirely. Then there was silence, the great silence of a place where no cars honk, no dogs bark, and no children play.

A small group of men had been standing together listening. When the plane could no longer be heard, the group broke up. The men spread out on the long glittering glacier high in the mountains of Alaska. Their link with the outside world was gone. It was time to get back to work, probing the secrets of the glacier.

This work was an important part of the International Geophysical Year, which began in July 1956 and ended in December 1958. The purpose of I.G.Y. was to explore the earth and its atmosphere with modern scientific methods.

During I.G.Y., hundreds of scientists lived and worked on glaciers. This work took them to the far corners of the world, to the cold and lonely places where earth's living glaciers lie. It took them to the mountains of Alaska and India, to the icecaps of Greenland and Antarctica.

It will be some time before all their findings can be put together and given meaning. But in the 18 months of I.G.Y., glaciers were given the most thorough study in history.

In Antarctica, men pitted themselves against the world's coldest weather to explore regions no one had seen before. In the mountains, men scaled the face of glaciers and climbed down into deep crevasses. From time to time, a small plane or helicopter would drop down out of the sky, bringing mail and supplies. When it took off, the men were once more alone on the vast and silent ice.

Perhaps the loneliest, coldest men were those who lived on the ice islands in the Arctic. Driven by winds and currents, these islands of ice float around the Arctic Ocean. Four of these islands became scientific stations during I.G.Y. Two were American and two Russian.

One U.S. station was the floating island called T-3. Big, sturdy, and 150 feet thick, T-3 had been used for research before.

The other U.S. ice island, Drift Station A, was two square miles in area, but only a few feet thick. (See photograph, page 63.)

Summer was the worst season on the ice islands. The summer sun melted the upper surface of the ice. The men lived in a flood of melt-water. Neither planes nor helicopters could land.

Both Americans and Russians had trouble with polar bears, which boarded the islands and prowled the camps. Once a plane was heading for the U.S. ice floe to drop supplies. The men tried to turn on their runway lights. Nothing happened—a playful bear cub had knocked over every light.

Large polar bears are dangerous. But so is the very ice in a floe. It can break up. This is just what happened to Drift Station A toward the end of I.G.Y.

The Americans were drifting through winter darkness near the North Pole. Suddenly they heard a noise like an express train rushing through their camp. Armed with flashlights, they hurried out into the dark and hunted. Soon they found it—a hairlike crack in the ice. The floe was about to split.

Quickly the men hauled their huts and supplies to a safer place half a mile away. A month or so later, the

floe split again. This time a rescue plane took the scientists and their records off the island. In their stay they had learned much about Arctic weather and about what happens to ice in summer and winter.

This information is just one small part of what I.G.Y. scientists wanted to learn about glaciers. For they are still seeking answers to some of the same questions that Agassiz worked on. The search has spread from the Alps to all the major glaciers in the world. It makes use of many new methods. Still, certain questions go unanswered. Others can be answered, but not quickly. They require years of work on many different glaciers.

How Does Ice Flow?

Let's start at the beginning. We know that some parts of the earth's surface are much colder than others. The Arctic and Antarctic are two of these places. The others are the heights of lofty mountains, for the higher the altitude the colder the temperature becomes.

In all these places there is snow the year round. Some of the snow melts in summer—but only some. So it is here that glaciers are found. If the rate of snowfall is

Every snowflake has six points.

greater than the rate of melting, glaciers grow. If the rate of melting is greater, glaciers shrink.

As we have seen, the weight of new snow packs down the old. As it is packed down harder and harder, the old snow turns to crystals of ice. And when the weight of ice becomes great enough, the glacier starts to flow.

Precisely how do ice crystals flow?

That is one of the questions without answers, though scientists have found out a good deal about the crystals.

A new snowflake has a beautiful crystal pattern and six fine lacy points. Under pressure, these snowflakes change. The points break off, melt, evaporate, or are crushed. So old snow is different from new snow. It takes the form of round granules, the shape of tiny grains of sand.

As still more snow piles up, pressure increases. Grains of old snow are packed more and more tightly together.

In time, they turn to ice crystals, which are also shaped like rough grains of sand. The crystals are packed together, forming rock-hard ice. As the glacier flows, the ice crystals are constantly being pushed out of shape and then re-forming. The stronger crystals become bigger. What started as a tiny grain may become a crystal as big as a basketball.

Like water, ice tends to flow downhill. It flows down mountains. It flows outward from the center of an ice-cap thousands of feet thick. The movement starts deep within the ice. And it is caused by the weight of the ice —that is, by the pull of gravity on the mass of ice. Ice crystals start at the head of a glacier and flow until they arrive at the melt line. That is the area where the ice melts and turns to water. (See photograph, page 58.) Meanwhile, other crystals have formed and taken their place in the glacier.

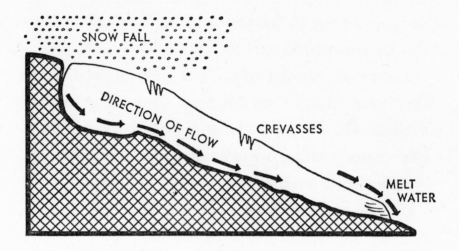

A glacier tends to flow downhill.

Now, when a glacier flows, the top layer of ice is likely to crack open because it is brittle. (See photograph, page 57.)

But ice deep within the glacier does not tear apart. Rather, the crystals keep regrouping themselves. How they do this is something geologists would very much like to know. Different geologists have different theories about it. But nobody knows whether one of these theories is the real answer.

One theory says that gravity causes the crystals to keep pushing against each other. In doing so, they push each other out of shape. When they have pushed and been pushed just so far, they regroup into new crystals. This movement accounts for the glacier's flow.

Another theory has to do with melting deep within the glacier. Pressure creates heat. And the great mass of snow and ice in a glacier creates heavy pressure. This causes melting within the glacier. Crystals then shift, flow, and refreeze.

Perhaps one theory is right. Perhaps both together are right. Perhaps neither is right.

Scientists working on this problem spend part of their time chopping out samples of ice. They take ice from the surface. They climb down a crevasse to get ice 100 or 200 feet below the surface. They drill into the ice and bring up cores from even farther down. Then they study the crystals in the samples, looking for changes that might give them the answer.

Measurements and More Measurements

Whatever the answer, glaciers do move. What scientists want to know is: How fast do glaciers move? Does the rate change from year to year? Do glaciers in different parts of the world move at the same rate?

Scientists know how to find the answers to these questions. But the answers require many measurements in many parts of the world over many years.

For example, a mountain glacier flows through a valley, reaching far up the walls. The center of the ice moves faster than the sides. Friction with the rocky walls of the valley slows the side movement. The surface of the ice may flow faster than the ice that is deep down—or it may flow more slowly.

Surface movement is measured by driving stakes into the ice, just as Agassiz did. The stakes are checked over a period of years. Changes show how fast the surface ice is moving. They show the different rates of center and sides.

Measuring flow 1,000 feet down in a glacier is harder. The best way to do it is by sinking a very long pipe in the ice and leaving it. The pipe will be carried along by the ice. If all the ice moves at the same rate, nothing will happen to the pipe. But suppose the deep ice moves faster than the surface ice. Then the deep ice will bend the lower part of the pipe forward. If the surface ice moves faster, the top part of the pipe will bend. The amount the pipe bends indicates the difference in the rates of flow.

How does a geologist sink a pipe 1,000 feet into the ice? He melts a hole for it, using a tool that's like a giant soldering iron. Melting such a hole may sound easy. But as any geologist can tell you, it's a long, hard job.

How much ice melts each year? That question also requires careful measuring year after year.

How thick is the ice? That's still another measuring job. But at least it's easier now than it was in Agassiz's time. Today it's usually done by setting off an explosion in the ice and recording what happens to the sound waves. Geologists know the rate at which sound waves travel through ice. When the rate changes, they know the ice has ended. The waves are passing through some other material, like bedrock. Scientists multiply rate by time. This gives them distance—the depth of the ice.

Some surprising answers turn up.

In certain places ice has proved to be flowing uphill. This happens where the bedrock of a valley does not slant downhill all the way. Where it slants upward, the glacier flows uphill.

In Antarctica, the ice turned out to be thicker than anyone had thought. In one place, it was 14,000 feet deep—nearly three miles!

What Plants Tell Us

Have the world's glaciers advanced at the same times? Have they retreated at the same times? These are questions for scientists who study plants—the botanists.

For example, a certain part of Chile is much like parts of Alaska and British Columbia. All have the same kind of mountains, the same climate, the same plants. In these areas, a number of glaciers are retreating. As they melt, they drop soil, rocks, and the remains of plants that they scooped up during their last advance.

Botanists search for the remains of trees that the glaciers knocked down and buried. The remains are dated by carbon-14 tests. This tells when the glaciers last advanced.

Living trees tell how long the glaciers have been retreating. The trees could not have taken root until the land was free of ice. And their age can be told by the number of rings in their trunks. So the age of the trees gives some idea of when the ice melted.

Botanists also search the rock piles of moraines, looking for ancient pollen. The pollen shows what kinds of plants used to grow in the region. And this, in turn, indicates what the climate was like.

When the reports come in from Chile, Alaska, and British Columbia, they are compared. Reports come in from other parts of the world. They are compared with the first ones. Comparisons show whether there is a pattern.

Frozen History

Another group of scientists examine questions of the past in a different way. They study the past by taking deep cores out of glacial ice. (See photographs, pages 60-61.)

A glacier contains hundreds of years of weather history, perfectly preserved in a "deep freeze." Here is the way this comes about.

Every summer the surface of the Greenland icecap melts. At summer's end, some of the melt refreezes in a thin crust. The yearly crusts mark layers in the glacier, and the layers are like the rings in a tree. Each one marks the glacier's growth for a year. This gives us information about the past, long before men were keeping weather records.

Something of this kind also happens in Antarctica, but its ice cores are harder to date. The layers are thinner and more closely packed; often there is little or no summer melt.

The ice cores reach far into the past.

Recently scientists brought up a long core of ice in Antarctica. The ice at the bottom had fallen as snow in the time of Charlemagne, more than a thousand years ago.

In Greenland, U.S. Army scientists drilled a core of ice 1,300 feet long. The layers in it showed that it was more than 800 years old at the bottom. From the thickness of the layers, scientists could tell how much snow fell in that area every year for 800 years. They also had samples of everything that fell with the snow— dust, meteorites, ash from great volcanic eruptions, fallout from modern atomic explosions.

Air trapped in ice forms bubbles. Bubbles in the Greenland core yielded samples of air from the time when Washington was at Valley Forge, when Columbus crossed the Atlantic, when King John signed the Magna Carta.

Analyzing what's in a huge ice core is slow work. And scientists will need to study a number of cores

A Greenland ice core dates back to the time of the Magna Carta.

before they are sure of their facts. But the deep freeze of weather promises a whole new source of information. It will be added to the finds of botanists and geologists. From the pooling of this information, we should learn much about ice and climate in the last thousand years.

This will be most helpful to the men studying to-day's glaciers and climate. They want to know: What weather conditions make glaciers grow? What conditions make them shrink? Why does snowfall vary? In what season do glaciers grow most? Why are some glaciers growing while most are shrinking?

Somewhere in the past and present there is a pattern. It may tell us what to expect of glaciers in the future.

What Glaciers Mean to Us

Glaciers affect every one of us. The reason has to do with water. Water is one of the few substances on earth that exist naturally as a liquid, a solid, and a gas. (You see it as all three—water, ice, steam—right in your own kitchen.)

Earth has some 350 million cubic miles of water. Far and away the largest part of this is in the oceans, with a smaller part in lakes and rivers. Only about 1 per cent is in the solid form of snow and ice. Even less than that is in the form of water vapor (gas) in the atmosphere. Yet there is a delicate balance here. Change the balance and man meets with catastrophe.

If all of today's glaciers melted, ocean levels would rise by at least 200 feet. Since most of the world's major cities are seaports, the rising ocean would swallow them.

Other areas would suffer a severe lack of water. Their rivers are fed by glaciers that melt in summer every year. Millions of people depend on this melt-water for their water supply.

Or suppose glaciers began to grow again. Then ocean levels would drop and seaports would become inland towns. Ice would creep down from the north, swallowing land and sending the breath of winter ahead.

Which way are we going? The truth is that we don't know, for our age is an odd one.

Scientists think that earth has been free of glaciers during most of its history. But several times, glaciers have formed and grown. The result has been an ice age. Our age is odd because we do have glaciers but we aren't covered by ice.

Most scientists agree that, in a sense, we are still in the Ice Age. The glaciers have retreated, but have not melted completely. There agreement ends. Some scientists take this as a sign that we are moving into a much warmer period. Others believe that ice will once more invade the Northern Hemisphere.

The one thing we do know is that changes are taking place in the world's glaciers.

For the past hundred years, most of the world's glaciers have been shrinking. The cause is a slow warming up of world climate, which has reached into polar regions. In the past 50 years, Spitzbergen (in the Arctic) has warmed up almost ten degrees. Little America (in the Antarctic) has warmed up five degrees.

Shrinking glaciers mean rising seas, which threaten to flood low-lying land areas.

Warmer temperatures are also melting the Arctic sea ice. If this continues, the Arctic Ocean may be open to shipping in another 40 years.

This kind of evidence leads some scientists to predict a warm, wet future for the world. The Ice Age will end, they say. And the world will have the same warm climate that it had a million years ago.

Yet during I.G.Y. scientists made a surprising discovery. Some of the world's big glaciers are not shrinking. On the contrary, they are growing. They grow fastest in summer. And they are growing *because* ice on the Arctic Ocean is melting.

Summer winds sweeping over the Arctic Ocean pick up lots of moisture. When the winds sweep over high glaciers, they strike cold. The moisture condenses and falls as snow. In winter, the Arctic Ocean is mostly frozen. Winds passing over it pick up only a little moisture. Little snow falls.

This may prove that glacier growth is caused chiefly

by moisture in the air. It may prove that a warming of climate can start an ice age.

Which scientists are right? The answer lies in the past. If we can find out *why* the Ice Age happened, we may also learn what the future holds for us.

7

The Sun, a Greenhouse, and a Wandering Planet

What could have caused more than a quarter of all the earth's land to be covered with ice several thousand feet thick? And what could then cause all this ice to melt?

These questions have long fascinated men. For more than a hundred years, they have sought the answers. The search has taken them far away from glaciers. It has taken them into a study of the sun, a study of the atmosphere, a study of the earth's crust. Some have thought we will never know the secret of the Ice Age until we learn how our planet was born. For the Ice Age was not a freak accident. It is somehow connected with the whole story of our planet.

So far no one has been able to prove what caused the Ice Age. But there are many different theories. Each was developed in the same way. Scientists started with known facts about the Ice Age. Then they tried to build a theory that would explain these facts.

They knew that hundreds of thousands of years ago a change occurred. As a result, glaciers began to grow and spread. They grew for thousands of years. And for thousands of years the land lay under massive sheets of ice. Then another change occurred. The ice melted, and glaciers retreated to the polar regions and the mountains. And it seems that this happened four times in the last million years.

The warm climate of a million years ago vanished. When ice and cold invaded the Northern Hemisphere, they made sweeping changes in the life that land supported.

That was the Ice Age. But Ice Age theories must go

far beyond it. They must explain certain other facts as well.

In addition to the Ice Age of the last million years, they must explain the ice ages that took place *hundreds of millions* of years ago. Geologists are sure there was an ice age about 230 million years ago and another one about 500 million years ago. Some think that still other ice ages may have occurred in the distant past. The earth has changed so much in those millions of years that we know very little about the earlier ice ages. But the marks of their glaciers prove they occurred. So they, too, must be explained.

Then, of course, the theories must explain the long periods when there were no ice ages. That is, suppose the cause of the ice ages is found. What stopped it from creating ice ages during the periods when there were none?

As you can see, the problem is a difficult one. And where do you look for the answer? Should you look for changes on the earth itself? Or should you look for changes beyond the earth—in its atmosphere or in the sun?

Through the years, all of these possibilities have been thought about. Many theories have been built around them and carefully worked out in great detail. It would be impossible to describe all the ice-age theories in just a few chapters. So, to see the great variety of ideas, we will take just a sampling of theories and go over them very quickly in this chapter and the next. Then we'll take a longer look at a new and different theory.

Many ice-age theories have to do with the sun, for the sun is the source of earth's heat. Just a small change in the amount of heat we receive from the sun would cause tremendous changes on the earth. It would be enough to melt all the ice in the world—or to freeze water that is now open.

Could such changes have caused the ice ages? Many scientists believe they could—and did. Some of these scientists think the changes stemmed from the sun itself. Others think the cause lies in the earth's atmosphere or in the earth's movement around the sun.

Changes in the Sun

The sun is a large globe of gases that continuously radiates heat and light. No one is sure just how the sun came into being. But many scientists think it was born as a great swirling cloud of dust and gas. As the cloud swirled, the gases packed themselves tighter and tighter. Then, perhaps 4½ billion years ago, the sun began to glow. The tremendous pressure at its core had triggered atomic fires. The nuclei of hydrogen atoms began combining and turned into helium. In this unending process they released great quantities of energy.

This process is called fusion. And it is what takes place in the explosion of an H-bomb.

Each second, the sun changes 564 million tons of hydrogen into 560 million tons of helium. Four million tons of matter are left over. These are converted into energy—equaling the energy of 4 billion H-bombs. This energy is shot into the solar system as light, heat, and invisible radiation.

We know that the sun's heat and light have been steady enough to support life on earth for millions of years. But some scientists believe the amount does vary over very long periods of time. It remains steady enough to support life, they say. But it also decreases enough to cause ice ages.

One of these scientists is Dr. E. J. Opik, director of the Armagh Observatory in Northern Ireland. Dr. Opik believes that changes in the sun's radiation must have caused the ice ages. He has made long and careful studies of the sun. He says that the vast fiery "furnace" of the sun cannot always produce the same amount of energy. Sometimes it produces less. When this happens, the earth grows colder—cold enough to cause an ice age. Dr. Opik says that the sun's energy decreases at intervals of several hundred million years. His findings indicate that decreases happened at the same times the ice ages did. (This would mean that earth is now moving into a warm period, like that of a million years ago.)

The theory does not explain the advances and retreats of glaciers during an ice age. Dr. Opik believes they may be caused by the "flickering" of the sun. This is a very complicated matter, but he thinks it may be related to sunspots.

Sunspots appear as pairs of darkish patches on the face of the sun. No one knows exactly what sunspots are or how they form. But they are cooler than the surrounding surface of the sun. Being less hot, they do not glow as brightly. That is why they look dark. Sunspots occur in cycles that average 11½ years. At the beginning of the cycle there are very few sunspots. By its end there are many sunspots.

A number of scientists believe that sunspots affect

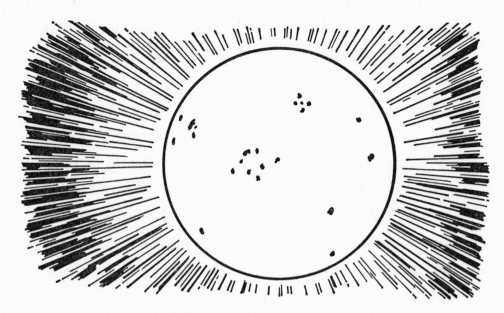

Sunspots are cooler than other areas on the sun's surface.

earth's climate. Some think that the earth warms up in periods when sunspots are many. They think it cools off when sunspots are few. They can't be sure, because our records of sunspots and weather do not go back far enough. But certainly our climate does go through short cycles of warming up and cooling off. Dr. Opik thinks a change of this sort might explain the advances and retreats of glaciers.

Other scientists raise a number of questions about this theory.

For one thing, they say, we have no way of checking

91

it. We have no record of the sun's brightness over the past million years, far less over the past 500 million years.

Also, nothing we know about the sun seems to support the theory. Recorded changes in the sun's radiation are very small. They last only for short periods of time.

It would take a major change in the sun to cause an ice age. The change itself would take millions or billions of years to come about. And it would have to last for thousands of years. We have no evidence that changes of this sort take place in the sun.

On the other hand, we can't prove they don't take place.

Then there's another and very different theory based on changes in the sun. This one was developed by a British scientist, Sir George Simpson.

He believes that the ice ages were caused by an *increase* in the sun's radiation. He explains the theory this way:

Warmer temperatures would cause an increase in cloudiness and in rain and snow. (Warmer air carries more moisture.) More snow would fall at the poles.

Under cloudy skies, it would not melt much. Glaciers would grow and an ice age would begin.

There is much more to the theory. But this is enough to give an idea of how much difference there can be in two theories dealing with changes in the sun.

As with the first theory, there is no way this one can be proved. Also, other scientists have a criticism of this theory. They say snow can build up only where the temperature is near freezing. When world temperatures rise, the areas where glaciers can form grow smaller and smaller. An ice age, they say, would be impossible.

The Greenhouse Effect

This theory also has to do with the sun's heat. But it rests on changes in the earth's atmosphere, rather than changes in the sun. The sun's heat and light pass through the atmosphere. Changes in the atmosphere can affect them.

If you have visited a greenhouse, you know that the temperature is much warmer inside the greenhouse than out of doors. Even if the greenhouse is not steam-heated, it's still warmer. The reason has to do with the glass in the roof.

The glass roof allows the sun's heat and light to pass freely into the greenhouse. The plants and other materials absorb this heat. After a while they, in turn, begin to give off heat. They give it off in the form of invisible rays called infra-red. These rays cannot pass freely through glass. They are trapped in the greenhouse. Heat comes in and doesn't escape. That's why the greenhouse temperature is warmer than the outdoor temperature.

Earth's atmosphere acts like the greenhouse roof. Heat and light from the sun pass freely through the atmosphere. The earth absorbs this sunlight. Then it gives off heat in the form of infra-red rays and warms the air. The atmosphere tends to trap the infra-red rays. It holds the heat, rather than letting it escape into space. For this reason, the earth is much warmer than it would be without the greenhouse effect of the atmosphere.

Knowing this, many scientists have wondered whether a change in earth's atmosphere might have caused the ice ages. Suppose something destroyed or weakened the greenhouse effect. Earth would become much colder. Then suppose the greenhouse started to work again. Earth would warm up. Some scientists have built an ice-age theory around this idea.

They started by asking what could affect our greenhouse. How could the atmosphere change so that more infra-red rays escaped?

Well, infra-red rays are blocked by three substances in the atmosphere: moisture, ozone, and carbon dioxide. Of the three, carbon dioxide is the one most likely to change in quantity. And if there were less carbon dioxide, more heat would escape.

Part of the carbon dioxide comes from erupting volcanoes. Suppose that, for a time, very few volcanoes erupted. There would be less carbon dioxide in the atmosphere. More of earth's heat would escape. Earth's climate would cool. A colder climate means colder oceans. The colder the oceans are, the more carbon dioxide they absorb. As a result, there would be still less carbon dioxide in the atmosphere. Still more heat would escape. The earth and its oceans would grow colder yet. And this would go on and on until volcanoes again began erupting.

Most scientists agree that a change in the amount of carbon dioxide would certainly affect earth's climate. (In fact, it's possible that an increase is causing the present warming up of climate. The increase comes from the factories, cars, and buses of our modern age.) But they don't think this could explain the ice ages.

For one thing, we have no proof that volcanoes ceased erupting. Quite the opposite may be true. Volcanoes probably erupted much oftener when the earth was younger. Even if they had stopped, could that explain a climate change that lasted perhaps a million years? It seems very doubtful.

Erupting Volcanoes

In the late 1800's a small volcanic island in the Dutch East Indies erupted violently. It threw gigantic amounts of fine volcanic dust into the air. This dust reflected the sun's rays, bouncing them back into space, away from the earth. So some of the sun's heat was cut off. World temperatures dropped several degrees. They stayed down until the dust settled to earth years later.

Still another theory is based on eruptions of this sort. Suppose the earth went through a period of tremendous volcanic eruptions. All that dust in the air would cause the earth to become much, much colder. This could have started an ice age.

But this theory, by itself, doesn't explain the facts either. In the Ice Age, glaciers advanced for thousands of years at a time. Eruptions could not account for such a long advance.

A volcano sends dust and carbon dioxide into the atmosphere.

The Nearness of the Sun

Suppose we lay aside changes in the sun or in the earth's atmosphere. Could anything else affect the amount of heat earth receives from the sun? The answer is yes—earth's distance from the sun. And that is the basis of another theory. It has been developed by a Yugoslavian scientist, A. Milankovitch.

He believes that ice ages began at times when the earth was farther away from the sun and ended when the earth moved nearer the sun. Such movements take place over very long periods of time. They are caused by small but important changes in the earth's travels.

The earth travels around the sun in an orbit the shape of an ellipse. And the earth's axis is tilted at an angle to the orbit.

If the earth were the only planet, neither the orbit nor the tilt would ever change. But earth is not the only planet. It is affected by the gravitational pull of other planets, especially Jupiter and Saturn. As a result, the shape of the earth's orbit changes. So does the tilt of its axis. The changes are small, and they must be reckoned in tens of thousands of years. But they do affect earth's distance from the sun and the amount of heat the earth receives.

Astronomers can work out these changes for any time in the past. (They can also calculate them for the future.) This information has been compared with what we know about the ice ages. The result seems to show that ice ages occurred when the earth was getting less heat from the sun.

There is much to be said for this theory. But it also raises some big problems.

For one thing, scientists aren't sure that the decrease in heat is enough to cause an ice age.

For another, if the theory is true, there should have been more ice ages than there were.

There are many more theories concerning heat from the sun. But these few show how hard it is to form a theory that explains all the facts.

The scientists who believe in any one of these theories know it has weaknesses. But to them it seems the most likely theory. Perhaps, they think, new evidence will turn up and strengthen the theory. Or perhaps it needs to be combined with other theories. They can't tell unless they work on it and try to improve it.

The answer they seek may be right around the corner —or it may not exist. For still other scientists believe that the mystery of the ice ages will never be solved by studying the sun's heat. They think the answer lies in the earth itself.

8

A World Turned Topsy-Turvy

The big mystery of the ice ages contains several small mysteries.

For example, Agassiz found the marks of glaciers in Brazil. Other geologists have found similar marks in Australia, India, and central Africa. The glaciers that made these marks were part of ice ages that ended hundreds of millions of years ago. Even so, what kind of ice ages could they have been? How could glaciers have formed in the tropics, near the equator?

Magnolias grew in Greenland long ago.

Another mystery is just as startling. The polar regions of the world were once warm and tropical. Fossils prove that fig trees and magnolias grew in Greenland. There are vast beds of coal in the icy island of Spitzbergen; they prove the island was once heavily forested. Coal beds and fossils show that Antarctica was also once a forested land.

For many years, these strange finds puzzled scientists. How could they be explained?

There seemed to be only one possible answer. At some time in the past, other lands and continents must have been at the poles. Perhaps the earth rolled over. Perhaps the continents moved. Whatever the cause, a

Greenland today is a land of snow and ice.

great change took place. The tropics became icy, frozen wastes. And icy wastes became tropics.

It was an astounding answer, but it seemed the only one that could explain the facts. The trouble was that no one could say how this might have happened. No one could really explain how the poles and equator might have changed places.

In fact, there was no evidence that this had happened. Magnolias in Greenland and glaciers in Brazil—these were facts. But they did not *prove* a change had taken place in the earth. They simply indicated it might have.

For years the idea was talked about, then put aside, talked about, then put aside. And during this time, various scientists began to develop theories to explain it.

Drifting Continents

One of the most famous theories was developed some forty years ago by a German scientist named Alfred Wegener. He proposed the idea that continents drift. Very slowly, he said, they slide across the face of the earth. This meant that Antarctica, for example, had once been far north of where it is now. And it had then had a very different climate.

However, Wegener was not trying to solve the mystery of the ice ages with his theory. He was trying to solve a mystery having to do with plant and animal life.

At certain times in the earth's history, new species of plants and animals developed. Fossils show that each species appeared in different parts of the world at about the same time. How could this have happened?

Most scientists explained it by land bridges and by channels. Land bridges had linked the continents. Channels had linked the oceans. This meant that different species had not suddenly sprung up all over the world. Each had developed in one place. Then it spread across land bridges (if it was a land plant or animal) or through the channels (if it was ocean life).

This theory was fine for a time. But as the study of fossils continued, more and more bridges and channels became necessary. And biologists could not agree on where these links had been. Some claimed there must have been a land bridge in a certain place; others insisted an ocean channel had been there. Then there was another problem. What had become of all these land bridges and channels?

Wegener suggested that they had never existed. Instead, he said, millions of years ago the continents were arranged in a very different fashion. They were lumped together in one or two huge land masses. Then, as time passed, they drifted apart.

Such an idea had been suggested in the 1880's by an Austrian, Eduard Suess. Suess believed that, millions of years ago, there was a super-continent. It lay in the southern hemisphere and stretched three quarters of the way around the earth. Suess called this super-continent Gondwanaland. He used it to explain why certain rocks and fossils were found in both India and South Africa.

Wegener took up this idea. Studying a map of the world, he found he could fit the continents together like parts of a puzzle. It took a little bending and stretching. But, still, they did fit roughly together. He then drew another map of the world, as he believed it had looked millions of years ago. North America and Europe were joined. South America, Africa, India, and Australia formed Gondwanaland.

To explain how the continents had drifted apart, Wegener drew partly on geology and partly on his own knowledge of climate.

Geologists had explained that continents "float" on softer matter beneath the earth's crust. They also knew that land masses rise and fall over long periods of time.

Wegener himself knew that earth's rotation affects the direction of moving air masses—that is, of winds.

So he argued this way. If continents can move up and down, they can also move sideways. They would tend to move in the directions the major winds do and for the same reasons. In this way, he described the continents as floating through the ocean flooring, much as icebergs float through the sea.

He "tested" his theory against what was known about world climates in much earlier times. Could it explain glaciers in the tropics? Forests in the polar regions?

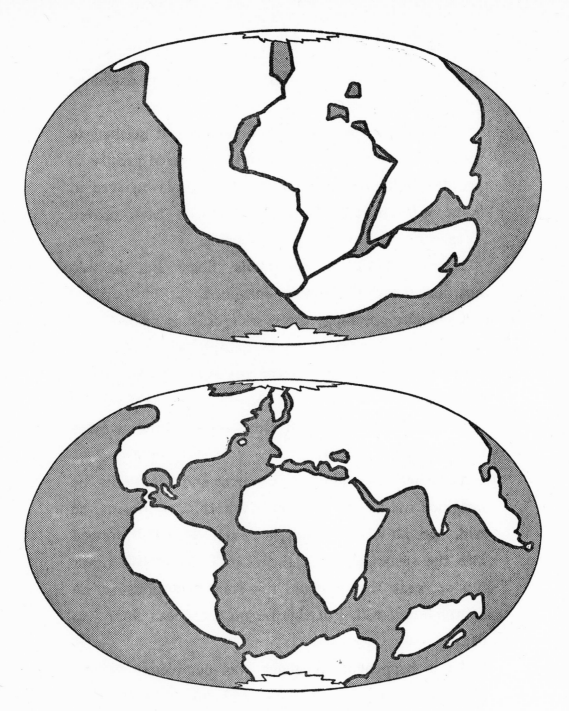

Some scientists believe that a great land mass (above) drifted
apart into continents (below).

Wegener decided it did. Drifting continents explained great changes.

Wegener's theory was very popular. It seemed to solve a variety of problems. And it appealed greatly to people's imagination. A great many people believed it. Some still do today, though geologists have proved Wegener's reasoning to be impossible.

It is quite true that continents "float." But they do not float the way Wegener imagined.

Generally speaking, the earth's crust is made up of two different types of rock: granite and basalt. The continents are granite; basalt lies under most of the ocean floors. The granite and basalt are strongly welded together. And they both float on a softer, weaker material below the crust.

Wegener knew about the granite and basalt. But he imagined the basalt was very weak. The continents, he said, had plowed through it. Then the basalt flowed into the spaces between them. In fact, he said basalt was so weak that it could not resist any pressure, no matter how small. For this reason the ocean floor was flat.

As it happened, Wegener was completely wrong

about basalt. It is much stronger than granite. The continents could not possibly have plowed through it. In addition, the ocean floor is far from flat. It is rugged land with great chains of undersea mountains and plateaus.

Even so, some serious scientists believe there is truth in the idea of drifting continents. They scoff at Wegener's explanation. But they do believe that the continents once formed a single land mass. How did the continents drift apart? Some scientists suggest that changes in the soft material under the earth's crust caused the drift. Some believe that the earth's core has expanded in the last 4½ billion years; this, they say, would force changes in the crust.

Most scientists, though, think drifting continents are impossible. If they are right, what other explanation could there be? How can we explain magnolias in Greenland and glaciers in Brazil?

Well, suppose a different kind of change took place. Suppose Brazil was once a polar region and Greenland was a tropical one. Then suppose the earth or its crust shifted. The Arctic Ocean moved to the North Pole; Antarctica moved to the South Pole. The shift would turn Greenland into an icy waste and Brazil into a tropical land.

At first glance this idea seems fantastic. Yet new evidence suggests that such a change did indeed take place. The evidence is "fossil magnets."

The Magnetic Poles

Since ancient times men have puzzled over magnets and their power. The Greeks knew that a strange stone from the land of the Magnesians could attract iron filings. Later, men discovered that a magnetized needle would point north. Nobody, though, knew why.

In the 1600's a famous English scientist, William Gilbert, made many experiments with magnets. He couldn't explain them either. But he did decide that the earth itself must be a huge magnet.

This, as you know, has proved true. And that's why we talk of two north poles and two south poles. There's the geographic North Pole and South Pole. Near the geographic poles lie the magnetic poles. Your compass points to the north magnetic pole.

How is the earth magnetized? What makes it a giant magnet? Modern scientists are still working on these questions. Among them is an English scientist named S. K. Runcorn.

A few years ago, Runcorn discovered millions upon millions of "fossil magnets" in the western United States. They had once been grains of iron that flowed from the earth in boiling lava. Apparently they had turned toward the magnetic north pole, lining up like so many compass needles. When the lava cooled and hardened, the line-up of iron grains was "frozen." Further study turned up fossil magnets in many parts of the world.

The discovery of fossil magnets was interesting. But the way they lined up was still more interesting. None of them pointed to the present north magnetic pole.

Runcorn studied the fossil magnets. He worked out the ages of the rocks in which they had been found. Then he made a chart of his findings. It showed the locations of the magnetic north pole as something like this:

> 600 million years ago: off the California coast
> 500 million years ago: in the middle of the South Pacific
> 200 to 300 million years ago: on the coast of Asia

Runcorn's discovery was of great interest to scientists trying to solve ancient mysteries of the earth's history.

Some, after a good deal of study, decided the fossil magnets didn't really mean anything. After all, they said, earth's crust has changed many times in all those millions of years. There's no telling where the fossils originally pointed. For all we know, they may have pointed where compass needles point today.

But many scientists believe the fossil magnets *are* evidence of gigantic changes on earth. Through the ages, different parts of the world may have lain at the poles. They reason this way:

The geographic and magnetic poles have probably never been far apart. That is, the South Pole has never been far from the south magnetic pole. And the North Pole has probably never been more than a few hundred miles from the north magnetic pole. This means that 500 million years ago the South Pacific lay at the North Pole. At that time, regions we know as tropical were icy wastes. Today's polar regions were warm and pleasant lands.

Then, over 500 million years, great changes occurred. As a result, the South Pacific moved into a warm area, and the Arctic Ocean moved to the North Pole. Antarctica moved to the South Pole. At the same time, other areas were also moving from warm climates to cold and from cold to warm.

The forests of Antarctica and Spitzbergen were buried under polar ice and snow. So were the fig trees and magnolias of Greenland. In now tropical lands, glaciers melted and vanished.

This topsy-turvy picture of the world is so strange that it's hard to take in. But you can demonstrate it for yourself.

Take a large ball of clay as the earth. Mark a line around the center for the equator. Pierce the ball through the North and South Poles with a knitting needle. The needle stands for the earth's axis. A lamp takes the place of the sun.

Remember that the axis is not straight up and down. It is at an angle to the sun. Hold it that way, and you have the earth as it is in the solar system. It rotates on its axis once a day. It revolves around the sun once a year. Notice how the North Pole is turned away from the sun for part of the year and how the South Pole is turned away for the rest of the year.

Now, suppose a great change takes place over millions of years. The result is a 90 degree shift in the earth.

Keep the axis as it is. But force the ball of clay around a quarter turn. The equator line is now pierced by the knitting needle. (Squeeze together the breaks in the clay. The earth's axis is an imaginary line and could not tear the earth apart.)

Again make the earth travel its yearly path around

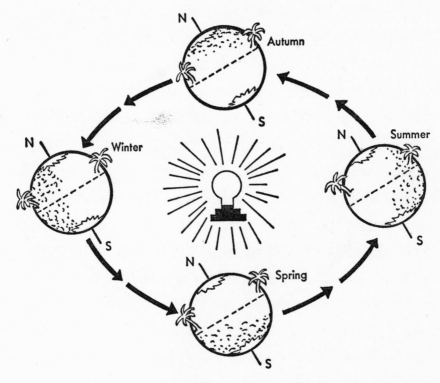

Some scientists believe that other parts

the sun. Lands that were at the equator are now at the North and South Poles. The former polar lands are at the equator, where they get the full warmth of the sun.

Snow and ice change to jungle, and jungles turn to snow and ice.

It seems unbelievable. Yet fossil magnolias lie beneath Greenland's ice. Brazil bears the marks of glaciers. And the fossil magnets point in many directions.

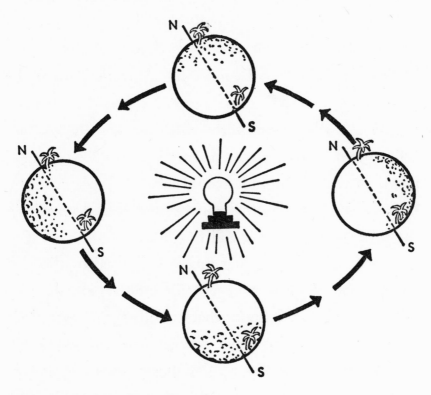

of the earth once lay at the poles.

How It May Have Happened

How could one area move to the North Pole while another moved away? Many scientists have worked on this question. And they suggest two possible answers.

One is that the whole earth rolls over.

The other is that the earth's crust shifts.

These two theories are alike in many ways, as you will see. But let's start with the one that says the whole earth rolled over.

The rolling over of earth would be much like the experiment with the ball of clay and the knitting needle. Earth's axis would remain the same. But the earth would roll around it. Lands that had been at the poles would move away. Other lands would take their place.

Some scientists say that shifts of material deep within the earth could make it roll this way.

Others think the rolling might be caused by changes on the face of the earth.

For example, we know that at different times whole chains of mountains have risen, thrust up from the earth's crust. We know that vast icecaps form in polar regions. Mountains and icecaps are both very

116

heavy. When new ones form, a great weight is added to the earth's surface. The weight might affect the earth's spin.

Look at it this way. Suppose a spinning top stands for the earth. If you glue a weight to some part of the top, what will happen? The top will still spin, but it will spin with a wobble. In the same way, a piece of clinging mud makes a ball wobble in flight. The top (or ball) seems to be trying to throw itself to one side.

This, certain scientists say, is just what happens to the earth when a great weight builds up on its surface. The weight puts a wobble in the earth's spin. The earth then slowly starts to roll. It keeps on rolling until it reaches a position where its spin is again in balance.

You can get an idea of this process if you cut out a roughly shaped circle of cardboard. Stick a pin through it and spin the cardboard. It will wobble in its spin, heaving in one direction. Move the pin toward the part of the circle that heaves. Spin it again. Keep moving the pin and spinning. Sooner or later you'll find the right place for the pin. There the cardboard will spin in perfect balance.

That, some scientists believe, is what the earth does. It slowly moves about its axis until it spins in balance.

Everyone agrees that if the earth wobbles and rolls, all this must happen very slowly. It might take millions of years for the weight to build up and cause a wobble. It might take millions of years for the earth to roll until it was again in balance.

But not everyone agrees that such a thing is possible. Most scientists state flatly that no known weight is great enough to make the whole earth roll over. And they do not believe that changes deep within the earth could make it roll either.

Of these scientists, a number believe in a somewhat different theory. They think that only the earth's crust shifts. They think that from time to time various forces cause it to slide over the layers below. As seen from space, it would look as if the whole earth were rolling. But actually only the crust would be moving.

This theory is based on what we know about the inside of the earth.

As far as we know, the center of the earth is liquid. This core is about 4,000 miles in diameter. It is probably made of iron that, under great pressure, has turned to liquid.

Outside the core are three main layers. The innermost is a solid shell, several hundred miles thick, called the

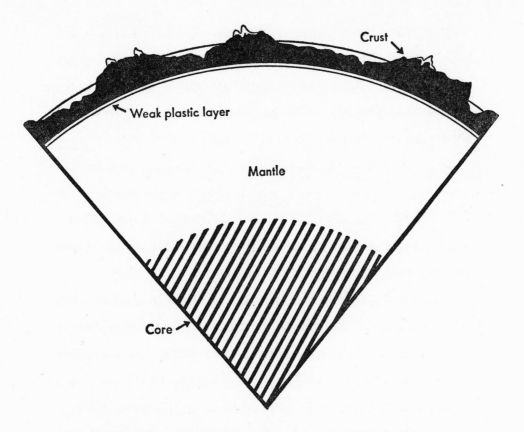

The earth's core is believed to be surrounded by three layers.

"mantle." Next there is a thin, weak shell, made of a sticky material that flows; it is described as "plastic." Finally, there is the earth's crust, which is 20 to 40 miles thick.

A slow flow of material within the earth may cause the crust to slide over the weak, plastic layer.

Or perhaps the cause lies on the surface of the earth.

119

The growth of a mountain range or an icecap would add weight to one part of the surface. As the earth rotated, the crust would tend to heave, as if it were trying to throw itself to one side. Then the crust would shift until the earth's spin was again in balance.

The Fact Test

If the earth rolls about or the crust shifts, this would explain many ice-age mysteries.

It would explain the marks of ancient glaciers in what we know as tropical lands.

It would explain why forests once grew in Antarctica and on Spitzbergen.

It would explain certain animal mysteries, because whole continents would have moved into different climate zones.

The change, if it took place, was slow. But it went on and on. Some animals could not adapt, and they died out. Some migrated. But they could go just so far. There the land ended. And there they had either to adapt or to perish.

Some animals appear to have died under strange circumstances. For example, fossil remains of animals

120

that loved warmth seem to show that these animals were trapped in the ice. Since the ice advanced slowly, this is puzzling. How could they have been trapped? But the puzzle is solved if the whole land was moving north. The animals could have died in a warm land that later became a cold land. This would make it appear that the animals had lived farther north.

Or there is another possible explanation. If the earth's crust shifted, this might have triggered many volcanic eruptions. Eruptions hurl vast quantities of volcanic dust into the air. The dust cuts off part of the sun's heat. It also causes more snow (or rain); moisture in the air condenses around the dust particles and falls to earth.

If this happened, the earth suffered a sudden drop in temperature. Snow fell in howling blizzards—and perhaps kept falling for years. It fell, too, in areas that had been sunny and warm. Cold and snow struck so quickly that many animals could not escape.

A change like this might even explain the mystery of the frozen mammoths.

In the past few hundred years, many woolly mammoths have been found perfectly frozen in the ground of Alaska and Siberia. It's as if they had been popped into a giant deep freeze. They were so perfectly pre-

Woolly mammoths may have been trapped in a sudden blizzard.

served that men could eat their meat. The mammoths' stomachs contained their last meal—flowers and grasses. The meal was also perfectly preserved. What happened to the mammoths? How could they have eaten flowers and then suddenly been frozen?

We know that woolly mammoths loved cold. We know that they lived near the edge of the ice sheets. Were they trapped in a summer blizzard and then swallowed by the ice sheet? We can only guess, but it does seem possible.

Earth's shifting crust would explain many mysteries of the ice ages. An earth that rolls about would also explain some of them. But, like all ice-age theories, these have their weaknesses.

As you remember, most scientists simply do not think the whole earth could roll about.

A number do think the crust shifts. But this is simply an idea. So far, no one has been able to prove it true or false.

There is another problem, too. The shifting-crust theory explains why ice ages have occurred in different parts of the world. But it does not explain the ice ages themselves. It does not explain why there were four great advances and retreats of glaciers in the last million years. Why should glaciers start to grow? Why should they melt and retreat?

In recent years, two American scientists have done a great deal of work on these questions. They accepted the idea of earth's shifting crust. But they wanted to know what caused the Ice Age.

They believe they have found the answer. And if they are right, it is of great importance to us. For their theory shows that we are nearing the start of another ice age.

9
The Coming
Ice Age

The theory of the coming ice age began with one clue. The clue stirred an idea in the minds of two scientists, Maurice Ewing and William L. Donn. And the idea led them over many strange trails and into many branches of science. At the end of the trail they came to this conclusion: The cause of an ice age is *not* a cooling of climate; the cause is a warming of climate, which melts the Arctic ice.

Our climate has been warming up. Ewing and Donn

predict that the warming, if it continues, will trigger a new ice age. The great glaciers of the north will again grow, and in growing they will reach out to swallow large chunks of North America and Europe.

This process, they say, has already begun. And a few hundred years from now, people may see the beginning of the next ice age.

The Trail of Clues

The first clue turned up in the summer of 1953, and it came from the bottom of the sea. It was found by an expedition that Dr. Ewing headed.

Dr. Ewing is director of Columbia University's Lamont Geological Observatory. Lamont has a three-masted schooner, the *Vema*. This ship is used for scientific exploration of the oceans.

In the summer of 1953, the *Vema*'s crew was using a "deep sea corer." This is a sharp-edged steel tube. Forced into the sea bed, it brings up long cores of sea bottom. The cores are sediment—matter that settled to the bottom. Naturally, the deeper the corer goes, the older the sediment it brings up. Sixty feet down, the

sediment is thousands of years old. In it, perfectly preserved, are traces of animals, rocks, and plants of different ages. With carbon-14 tests, a fossil shell, for example, can be dated. Then there is a somewhat similar
test with oxygen-18, which acts as a built-in thermome-
ter. With oxygen-18 tests, scientists can read ocean
temperatures back through 600,000 years.

All through that summer, the *Vema*'s crew brought
up cores from the Caribbean, from Atlantic waters near
the equator, and from the Gulf of Mexico. The cores
showed an odd pattern. The top twelve inches of
sediment were pink. Then the color abruptly turned to
gray. Other scientists had reported the same pattern in
the North Atlantic.

What did the color change mean? Dr. Ewing found
out shortly after he got back to Lamont. The cores were
put through laboratory tests for oxygen-18 and carbon-
14. From these tests came two pieces of information.

(1) The color change showed a sudden warming of
the ocean. The gray sediment was colored by the shells
of tiny cold-water animals. Shells of tiny warm-water
animals colored the pink sediment.

(2) This sudden change took place 11,000 years ago.

Before that, for 90,000 years, the ocean had been much colder. And this was true of the whole Atlantic.

Dr. Ewing was baffled by the change. So was Dr. Donn, who teaches geology and who also directs research in weather and climate at Lamont. What could possibly have warmed the whole Atlantic so suddenly 11,000 years ago?

The problem was never far from their minds. One day a possible answer came to them. The answer had to do with ice. Ice is the only thing that can cause a big temperature change in water. When ice breaks up and melts or floats away, water warms up.

By and large, oceans don't freeze over. But there is one exception. That is the Arctic Ocean. Small and almost entirely surrounded by land, it freezes much as a large lake does.

Ewing and Donn wondered: What would happen if the ice went out of the Arctic Ocean? Suddenly they got a glimpse of what that might mean, and their minds leaped ahead. Here, perhaps, was an explanation of the Ice Age.

This is what they were thinking.

The Arctic Ocean is almost landlocked. But there is an opening between Norway and Greenland. It's a broad opening, but shallow. Here the cold Arctic Ocean and the warmer Atlantic meet. But they do not flow freely into each other because the meeting point is shallow.

Suppose the Arctic glaciers began to melt. This would raise the level of the Arctic Ocean. Then its waters would mix freely with those of the Atlantic. The Atlantic would become colder as the Arctic waters poured

The Arctic Ocean is almost surrounded by land.

into it, while the Arctic Ocean would become warmer. The Arctic Ocean would be so much warmer that it would not refreeze, even in winter. More important, there would be much moisture in the air over the Arctic Ocean—and, as a result, heavy falls of snow.

Heavy snowfalls in the north would build glaciers. As the snows kept falling, the glaciers would grow. For snow would build up faster than glaciers could melt. In fact, as long as the Arctic Ocean was open water, the glaciers would grow. The result would be an ice age.

Of course, this process wouldn't go on forever. In time, so much water would be locked up in glaciers that the level of the Arctic Ocean would fall several hundred feet. Its water would no longer mix freely with the warming Atlantic. As soon as this happened, the Atlantic would warm up and the Arctic Ocean would freeze.

With a frozen ocean, much less snow would fall in the Arctic. Glaciers would shrink, drawing back from lands to the south. And this would mark the end of the ice age.

In time, even glaciers in the Arctic would melt. Their water would drain back into the Arctic Ocean. The ocean level would rise. Again its waters would be warmed by the Atlantic. There would be heavy snowfalls. Glaciers would grow until they had lowered the level of the Arctic

Ocean. The ocean would freeze once more. And this cycle would be repeated time and again.

Was this the explanation of the Ice Age? Ewing and Donn thought it was. But they needed proof.

The Search for Proof

How could Ewing and Donn check their theory? The best way was to check it against known facts.

For example, there were the corings brought up by the *Vema*. The corings showed a sudden change in ocean temperature. The theory explained the change. While the Atlantic and Arctic oceans mixed freely, the Arctic would have cooled the Atlantic. When the two no longer mingled, the cold water was cut off. The Atlantic warmed up.

There was another way to check, too. They could work out "what would have happened if . . ." What, for instance, would happen to the world's weather if the Arctic Ocean were open water? Dr. Donn made a weather map of the world. An open Arctic Ocean, he found, would create a different storm pattern from the one we know. There would be more rain and snow in the Arctic. Winds would carry more moisture from the oceans to inland areas. Rain would fall on areas like the Sahara. Blizzards would sweep eastern North America.

But this was not enough. Ewing and Donn needed more evidence—and they got it. Some they found themselves. Some came from other scientists.

Pictures, Cores, and Caves

If their theory was true, then the Arctic Ocean had been open water. Did evidence of this exist?

Ewing and Donn read accounts of Arctic explorers. They found little to help them. Then, one day, they were going through some old magazines. They found a picture of an Arctic beach. It was the kind of beach that is formed by pounding waves over long periods of years. Here was one clue that the Arctic Ocean must have been open water at some time in the past. How else could the beach have been formed?

The theory raised another, even bigger question. If it was true, then the forward march of ice in North America must have ended at the precise time that the Arctic Ocean froze and the Atlantic warmed up. Could this be proved?

Two kinds of evidence were needed. One would show when the ice stopped advancing. The other would show when the Arctic Ocean froze and the Atlantic warmed up. And the evidence was there.

Dr. Libby's tests on fossil wood dated the end of the Ice Age. The date was 11,000 years ago.

A second piece of proof came from the cliff caves of Nevada and Utah. These cliffs tower far above the dry Great Basin of those states. They are marked by waves

When the floods of melt-water drained away, people moved into cliff caves.

that stirred long-vanished lakes. The lakes were formed by great rains that fell in the Southwest during the Ice Age.

Far below the wave marks are the cliff caves. When the great rains stopped, the lakes began to drain. The caves were exposed, and men moved into them. With nets and baskets they caught fish in the lakes. When the men moved on, they left old nets and baskets behind.

Carbon-14 tests showed the nets and baskets to be almost 11,000 years old. This was more evidence that glaciers began to retreat 11,000 years ago.

Other evidence showed what had happened in the oceans.

There were the pink-and-gray corings, which marked a change of ocean temperature 11,000 years ago.

Dr. Ewing had gone back to sea in the *Vema*. In the Gulf of Mexico, he found proof of a great rise in sea level. At that time the lower channels of the Mississippi had been drowned by a rising sea. Through corings, he dated the rise: 11,000 years ago. The cause of the great sea rise must have been melting glaciers.

As other evidence turned up, there could no longer be any doubt. The Ice Age had ended 11,000 years ago.

And at that same time the Atlantic had suddenly warmed up, while the Arctic Ocean became colder.

Ewing and Donn felt sure these facts were related, that they were cause and effect. The freezing of the Arctic Ocean had caused the end of the Ice Age.

They could make a good case now for their theory. But they wondered if it was good enough. Could other scientists find weaknesses in the theory and tear it apart?

By sheer luck, they stumbled on an exciting new clue. A friend told them that he had overheard an interesting conversation. It seemed that traces of ancient people had been found in the Arctic.

Ewing and Donn got to work. They learned that flint weapons had been found in the far North. In fact, the oldest flints in all North America had been found around the Arctic Circle. Other evidence seemed to show that thousands of years ago men had lived for generations in the Arctic.

This evidence had puzzled the scientists who study the development of man, the anthropologists. They knew that men had probably come to North America over a now-vanished land bridge between Siberia and Alaska. But why would these men have settled in the Arctic? What game would they have found to hunt

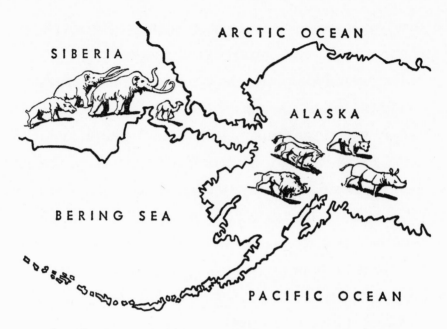

A land bridge probably connected Asia to North America.

around the Arctic Ocean? And why would these people have stayed there for generations?

If the Arctic was then a land of snow and ice, this was baffling. But suppose the Arctic Ocean had been open water, as Ewing and Donn believed. Here was the answer. Near the Arctic Ocean men could live. There would have been animals to hunt and fish to catch. In fact, the people could not have gone south. To the south lay towering walls of ice—the glaciers of the Ice Age.

There was still another clue. Anthropologists said

they were pretty sure men had suddenly migrated south about 11,000 years ago from the Arctic.

Ewing and Donn put the pieces together this way:

When the glaciers were growing, water from the oceans was locked up in ice. A land bridge appeared between Siberia and Alaska. Over this bridge ancient men migrated to North America. The Arctic was then much warmer than it is now because the Arctic Ocean was open and tempered the climate. The people could live there by hunting and fishing. They could not move south because of the ice.

Then, unknown to them, a great change took place. The Atlantic was cut off from the Arctic Ocean. The Arctic Ocean began to freeze, and the chill of ever-winter gripped the land around it.

For the people, the change must have been terrifying. Their home became much colder. Their food grew scant. The land bridge to Siberia vanished under a rising ocean; they could not go back.

Just at this time, openings appeared in the great walls of ice. Melting glaciers made it possible for them to flee south from the Arctic.

The problems that had bothered anthropologists greatly strengthened the Ewing-Donn theory.

Then one last clue fell into place. From the Sahara came word of cave paintings. Men had lived on what is now a desert and hunted animals on grassy plains during the Ice Age. Only rain could have made grassy plains out of a desert. Only an end to rain could have turned the plains into desert. And Dr. Donn's weather map showed just this. An open Arctic Ocean—heavy rain in today's deserts. A frozen Arctic Ocean—no heavy rains.

Two Big Questions

The Ewing-Donn theory deals with two other questions.

The first is: What started the Ice Age?

The two men believe that it was started by a shift in the earth's crust. The shift carried Antarctica to the South Pole. It carried the almost landlocked Arctic Ocean to the North Pole. This meant there was land in the two coldest regions of the earth. Snow fell on the land, built up, and changed to ice. As long as the Arctic Ocean was open, Arctic glaciers grew, causing the Ice Age. When the ocean level fell, the water grew cold and froze. Glaciers then retreated—until their melting again raised the level of the ocean.

The second question is: Will the melting of the Arctic glaciers start another ice age?

The answer is that, if the melting continues, it may well start another ice age. But we are not sure of what is happening to world climates.

In recent years, scientists have noted a distinct warming of climate.

The warming shows itself in many ways. In Iceland and Greenland, temperatures are up ten degrees. In Canada, land that only a few years ago was too cold for crops can now be farmed. In New York, the time has vanished when Long Island Sound and the Hudson River froze over in winter. Birds have changed their nesting grounds and moved north. Fishermen report that cold-loving cod have left Cape Cod for Newfoundland.

Warmer temperatures . . . melting ice . . . rising oceans. The sea level used to rise six inches every hundred years. Today it's rising at four times that rate. In Holland, old dikes no longer offer enough protection. Towns on the east coast of the United States have also felt the change. In bad storms, tides come higher than ever before.

The Hudson River formerly froze over in winter.

As the Atlantic's level rises, more and more warm water pours through the opening into the Arctic Ocean. And that small, cold ocean is definitely warming up. In the last 15 years, the area of its ice has shrunk 12 per cent. The ice is 40 per cent thinner.

Scientists have noted, marked, and measured these changes. But no one knows whether the present climate trend will continue.

New facts, new theories keep coming to light, for never before have so many scientists been studying glaciers and probing the mystery of the Ice Age. Just

140

Now our climate has warmed up.

recently one geologist, Dr. Richard J. Lougee, put forward a whole new idea of the Ice Age. He has been studying the marks of glaciers for some thirty years. And he has concluded that the ice came down not four times but only once during the Ice Age.

If he is right, then the Ice Age began much closer to modern times than anyone has thought. Many old ideas will have to be reworked. New light will be shed on theories of the Ice Age.

At present, though, the Ewing-Donn theory is believed to be the most likely explanation of the Ice Age.

Many scientists have tried to tear it apart. Nearly all have ended by believing there is some truth in it.

If Ewing and Donn are right, there will be a long-range warming up of climate. Glaciers will go on melting. Ocean levels will rise still higher.

Our problem then will be floods. They will be floods unlike any we have known in this country. The water will simply rise and come in over the land. There it will stay, taking more land each year. Perhaps some coastal cities could be protected by dikes. Others will have to be abandoned and their people moved inland.

Finally, the oceans will stop rising. For glaciers will be growing in the north—and taking water out of the sea.

The ice age will begin with a summer slush in certain parts of the north. For the first time in thousands of years, winter snows will last through the summer. The rate of snowfall will be greater than the rate of melting, and glaciers will grow.

Slowly—inch by inch, foot by foot—the ice crept southward. From the far north, great sheets of ice spread out, swallowing the land. From high mountains, rivers of ice reached down with frigid touch.

Is that just a description of the past? Or is it also a description of the future?

For the present we can only wonder. Perhaps today's scientists will be able to tell us what the future holds. Perhaps it will take another generation of scientists— your generation—to solve the mystery of the Ice Age.

Index

Index

Numbers in **bold-face type** refer to maps and illustrations.

Index

Index

Lewis Glacier (Kenya), **57**
Libby, Willard F., 48-51, 133
Little America, **62**, 82
Lougee, Richard J., 141

M

McCall Glacier (Alaska), **59**
Magnetic poles, 110-115
Mammoths, 34, 36, 43, **122**
  prehistoric paintings of, 38
  sudden death of, 121, 123
Melt line (of glaciers), **58**, 71, **72**
Milankovitch, A., 98
Moraines, 9, 11, 76
Mt. McKinley (Alaska), **53**
Muldrow Glacier (Alaska), **53**

N

North America
  and bridge to Asia, **136**
  ice sheet in, 19, **24-25**, 26
North Pole
  drift station near, 68
  and earth's axis, 113
  and earth's shifting crust,
    109, 115, 116, 138
  and north magnetic pole,
    110, 112
  surrounded by water, **23**
Norway, **127**, 128

O

Oceans
  and carbon dioxide, **95**
  floor of, 109
  level of, 28, 80, 142

Opik, E. J., 89-91
Oxygen-18, 127
Ozone, infra-red rays blocked by, 95

P

Paleontologists, 41
Polar bear, 67-68

R

Radioactive carbon, 48
Reindeer, 38
Rhinoceros, woolly, **34**, 38, 43
Rhône River, 8, 13
Rocks
  erratic, 5-6, **7**
  polished by glaciers, 9, 11, 19, **55**
Runcorn, S. K., 111-112
Russia, ice sheet in, 26

S

Saber-toothed tiger, 31, **35**, 36
  prehistoric paintings of, 38
Sahara, during Ice Age, 27, 138
Scandinavia, ice in, 23, 26, **29**
Shoup Glacier (Alaska), **56**
Siberia
  Alaska linked to, 27, 135,
    136, 137
  ice sheet in, 23, 26
  mammoths preserved in, 121, 123
  present-day tribesmen of, 40
Simpson, George, 92
Sloth, ground, 31, 35-36
Snow bridge, 14, **58**
Snowfall, 21-22, 69-70, **72**, 82, 130

About the Author of this Book

Patricia Lauber is a versatile author, for she is equally at home writing fiction and non-fiction. As editor of a science magazine for young people, she has been in touch with the new and fascinating material being uncovered by scientists today. Although the Ice Age ended 11,000 years ago, she found much of her information in current periodicals, and even in a teletype dispatch from Washington.

Among Patricia Lauber's books of non-fiction are *St. Lawrence Seaway* and *Battle Against the Sea: How the Dutch Made Holland.* Three of her delightful stories for younger readers are *Adventure at Black Rock Cave, The Runaway Flea Circus,* and *Found: One Orange-Brown Horse.* A graduate of Wellesley College, she lives in New York City.

About the Illustrator of this Book

John C. Wonsetler, a well-known mural painter, is particularly interested in illustrating books for young people. He has provided the illustrations for three Landmark Books—*Up the Trail From Texas*, *Buffalo Bill's Great Wild West Show*, and *Rogers' Rangers and the French and Indian War*.